SHARING THROUGH SONG

I WILL TRUST IN HEAVENLY FATHER AND HIS SON, JESUS CHRIST—THEIR PROMISES ARE SURE

VOLUME TWO

SHARING THROUGH SONG

I WILL TRUST IN HEAVENLY FATHER AND HIS SON, JESUS CHRIST—THEIR PROMISES ARE SURE

VOLUME TWO

BY

ALISON PALMER

Horizon Publishers
Springville, Utah

ISBN: 0-88290-798-0
Order Number C3005
v.1

Published by Horizon Publishers,
an imprint of Cedar Fort, Inc.
925 N. Main Springville, Utah, 84663
www.cedarfort.com

Distributed by:

CEDAR FORT

Cover design by Nicole Williams

Printed in the United States of America
10 9 8 7 6 5 4 3 2 1

Printed on acid-free paper

Contents

Acknowledgments

Many thanks to Duane and Jean Crowther of Horizon Publishers for continuing to have faith in my work. I also extend great appreciation to Lee Nelson and Georgia Carpenter at Cedar Fort for allowing me to share my enthusiasm for this project with them.

I would like to thank Debra Stinson as well for her dedication and hard work creating the beautiful illustrations that add so much to my words.

I express thankfulness and love to my husband and children for loving me despite it all and picking up the pieces of life that I let slide while I'm engrossed in a manuscript.

Most of all, I must express my love and gratitude to my Heavenly Father. He continues to bless me. He filled my soul with the thoughts and ideas that became this book. Through his inspiration, may the lives of many children be blessed.

HOW TO USE THIS BOOK

Most of us have traditionally separated sharing time into a short lesson and a music time. We have been asked by the General Primary Board to use the full thirty to forty minutes for sharing time; music is integrated throughout. (See "Instructions for Sharing Time," *2006 Outline for Sharing Time and the Children's Sacrament Meeting Presentation*, 1.) This is not always easy. Compliance requires early preparation and more communication and cooperation between presidencies and choristers, but it works!

Music teaches where words fail, and if we do not merge the two, we are missing beautiful opportunities to teach our children things they will always remember. The overall goal of sharing time should be to teach the gospel and build testimonies. *Sharing through Song Volume Two* works on this philosophy. Children must first hear the gospel and then sing the gospel. When these two work together, they will feel the Spirit and know the gospel is true.

This manual is designed to help those who desire to follow the guidance of our leaders to the best of their ability. However, it has limitless potential. The lessons are built around inviting the Spirit through the use of scriptures and song. Please feel free to mold these lessons to fit your needs as a leader, teacher, or parent.

The lessons are set up according to the month they are assigned in the 2006 Outline. There are two lessons for each month. One lesson focuses on the message of the suggested song. The second lesson for the month focuses on a suggested topic from the outline with multiple songs used for reinforcement.

Please also keep in mind that this is copyrighted material intended for use within the purchaser's home or Primary only. If you enjoy using it, share that information with your friends, but allow them to show honesty by purchasing their own copy of this manual.

May the Lord bless you in your endeavors to serve His children.

1. SCRIPTURE POWER

Friend, October 1987, 10–11

Opening Song: "Seek the Lord Early," *Children's Songbook,* 108

Closing Song: "Scripture Power" *Friend,* October 1987, 10–11

MATERIALS NEEDED

- Copies of included illustrations
- One poster board
- Tape, sticky tack, or other fastener

PREPARATION

- Color and cut the illustrations. The armor could be used again in lesson two.
- Laminate all pieces for durability.

TEACHING SUGGESTIONS

Start with the boy previously fastened to the poster board with tape or your chosen fasteners. Tell the children that this boy has found a way that he can strengthen his testimony every day. Doing this one thing helps him feel happier and more peaceful and makes it easier to make right choices. Ask the children what they think this boy could do that would help him so much. Commend their answers and point out that the name of the song they will learn today is "Scripture Power." Let the children share their thoughts on how the scriptures can bless our lives in many different ways.

Introduce the phrases of the song, one at a time. Tell the children the words and show them the corresponding picture when appropriate. Have them repeat the phrase several times until they are fairly accurate with the wording. When they are able to repeat back the phrase proficiently, add that piece to the poster picture as outlined at the end of this lesson.

Teach the first verse and chorus; then introduce the accompaniment. When all the pieces are in place, review the words together while you point to each piece. Sing the song several times as the children help you point to the pieces of the picture.

Once the children have gained some confidence with the words and melody, introduce the second verse in the same manner. Repeat the entire song one verse at a time, and then sing it through in its entirety. As you review, help the children understand how the scriptures can affect their lives in the ways mentioned. Share your personal testimony of the scriptures with the children.

The children can also actively participate in the review process by popping up and down from their seats every time the word "scripture" is sung, or by raising their own scriptures over their head with the words "scripture power" in the chorus.

Special Note: This song offers a chance to extend any special challenges to the children: to bring their scriptures every week, to read daily, to memorize the scriptures listed in the program outline, or to read the entire Book of Mormon. Prayerfully consider if it is appropriate to extend any such challenge to your Primary children and prepare to do so in conjunction with this lesson.

SONG OUTLINE AND PICTURE PLACEMENT

Verse 1:

- "Because I want to be like the Savior, and I can"—picture of Jesus Christ to top right
- "I'm reading His instructions, I'm following His plan"—scriptures to bottom left
- "Because I want the power His word will give to me"—power to bottom right
- "I'm changing how I live, I'm changing what I'll be"—talk about changes you are making to the picture and the positive changes these things make in a person's life

Chorus:

- "Scripture Power keeps me safe from sin"—point to scriptures and power
- "Scripture Power is the power to win"—point to scriptures and power again
- "Scripture Power"—repeat pointing with each word
- "Ev'ry day I need the power that I get each time I read"—point to power first and then returning to the scriptures

Verse 2:

- "I'll find the sword of truth in each scripture that I learn"—add sword to boy's right hand
- "I'll take the shield of faith from these pages that I turn"—add shield to boy's left hand
- "I'll wear each vital part of the armor of the Lord"—add breastplate to boy's chest
- "And fight my daily battles, and win a great reward"—emphasize boy's overall appearance (ready for battle)

Repeat Chorus

ook
of
rmon
BIBLE

POWER

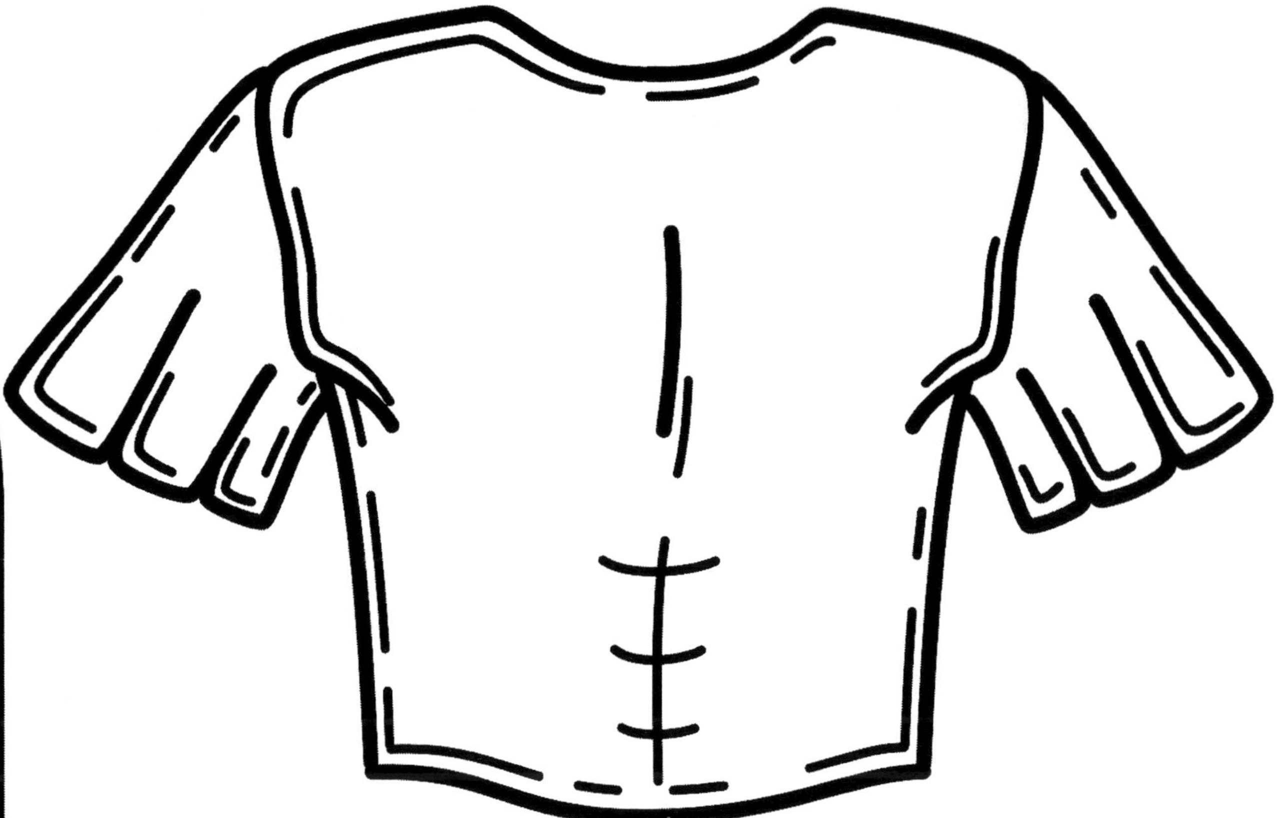

TRUTH

Faith

2. Armor of God Paper Dolls

Opening Song: "I Will Be Valiant," *Children's Songbook,* 162

Closing Song: "Army of Helaman," *Children's Songbook,* 172

Materials Needed

- Boy from "Scripture Power" lesson
- One copy of each large piece of armor from this lesson
- Copies of small paper doll and clothing for each child
- Scriptures for use by children
- Crayons or colored pencils for use by children
- Chalkboard or display area
- Tape or other fasteners

Preparation

- Color and cut the large pieces of armor.
- Write the scripture references listed on the following page on the back of the appropriate piece of armor.
- Laminate each piece of armor for durability.
- Review Ephesians 6: 11, 13–17 and the additional scripture references.

Teaching Suggestions

Read Ephesians 6:11, 13–17 with the children. Ask them what they think this group of scriptures is asking them to do. Remind them that they talked a little bit about these same things when they learned "Scripture Power" earlier. Tell them that today they will continue to talk about ways that living the gospel protects them from sin and other challenges they face everyday.

Post the large boy on the chalkboard or other display area. Identify each piece of armor and place the pieces to the side of the board as each one is listed.

Ask a reverent child to come up and choose a piece of armor to place on the boy. When a piece is chosen, ask the children what they think it means to have the quality, or gift, that each piece of armor identifies. Allow them to share their thoughts and then ask someone to look up the scripture on the back of that piece. Read the scripture together, clarify the children's thoughts, and bear testimony of each gospel principle. Let the child place the piece of armor on the boy and return to his or her seat.

Sing the corresponding song before moving to the next piece. Repeat this pattern until all the pieces of armor have been placed.

Pass out the paper dolls to the children for them to color with any remaining time. Encourage them to take their dolls home, cut them out and share what they have learned about the armor of God with their family during family home evening.

Armor, Scripture, and Song

- **Loins** (truth)—John 14:6 (testimony of the Savior)—"I Feel My Savior's Love," *Children's Songbook,* 74
- **Breastplate** (righteousness)—Alma 53:20–21 (true to commandments)—"I Pledge Myself to Love the Right," *Children's Songbook,* 161
- **Feet** (gospel of peace)—John 14:27 (the Spirit gives peace)—"Teach Me to Walk in the Light," *Children's Songbook,* 177
- **Shield** (faith)—Hebrews 11:1–3 (trusting God)—"Faith," *Children's Songbook,* 96
- **Helmet** (salvation)—3 Nephi 27:13–21 (plan of salvation)—"I Will Follow God's Plan for Me," *Children's Songbook,* 164
- **Sword** (Spirit/word of God)—2 Nephi 4:15–16 (delight in scriptures)—"Scripture Power," *Friend,* October 1987, 10–11

Righteousness

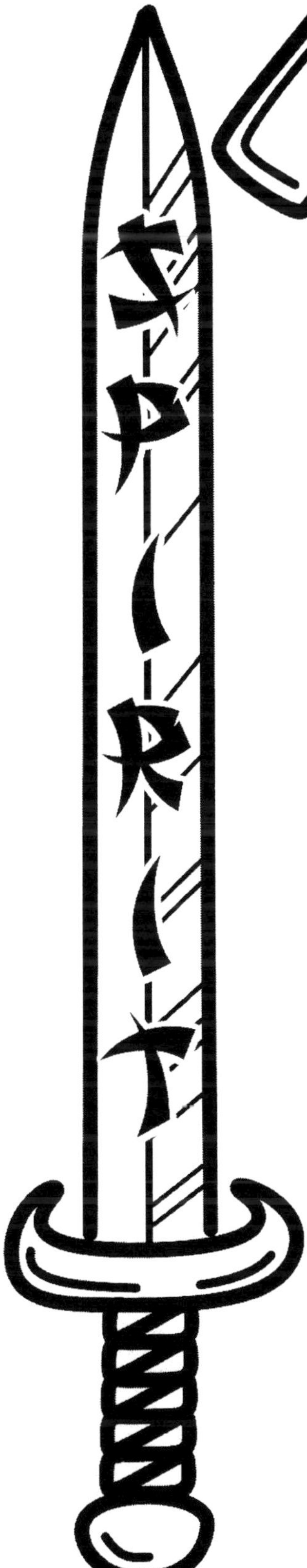
Spirit

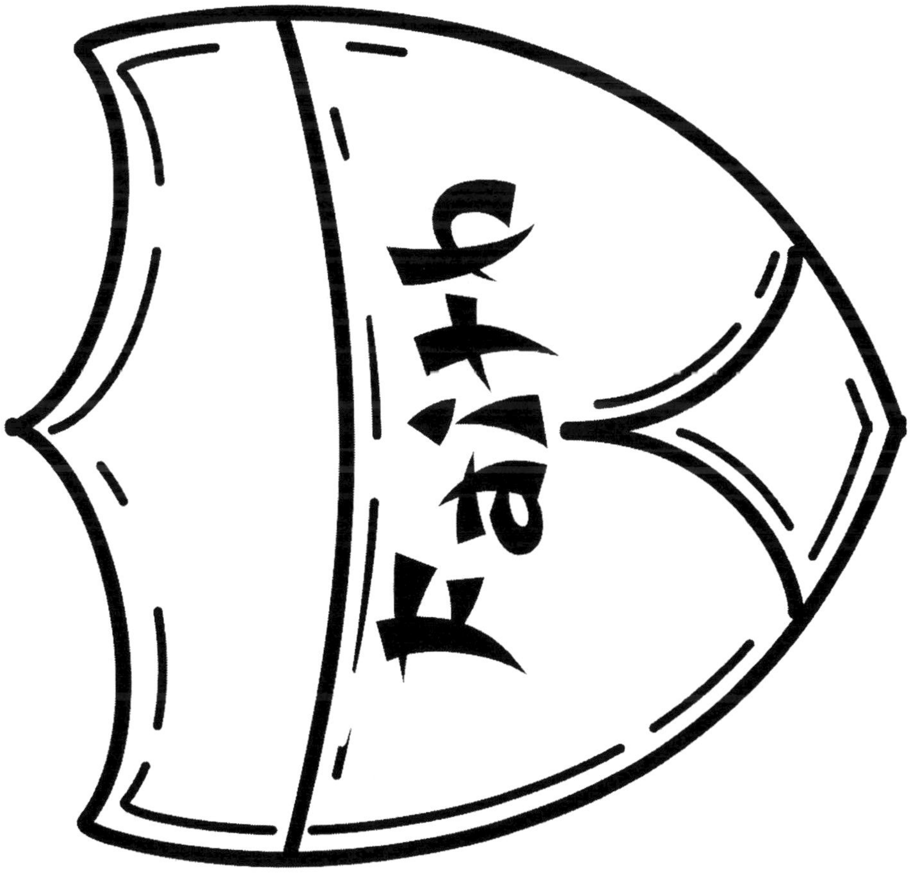
Faith

Truth

Salvation

Peace

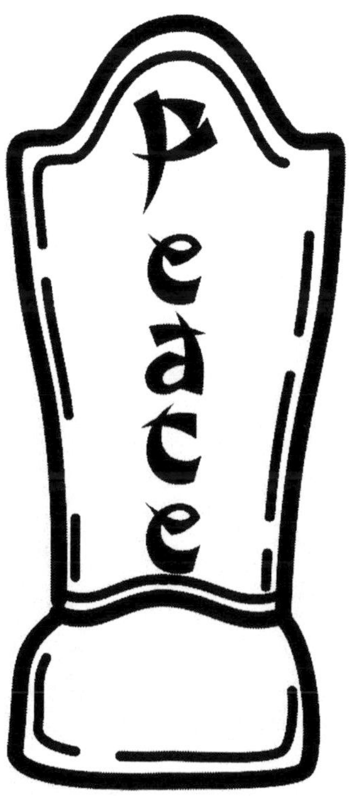
Peace

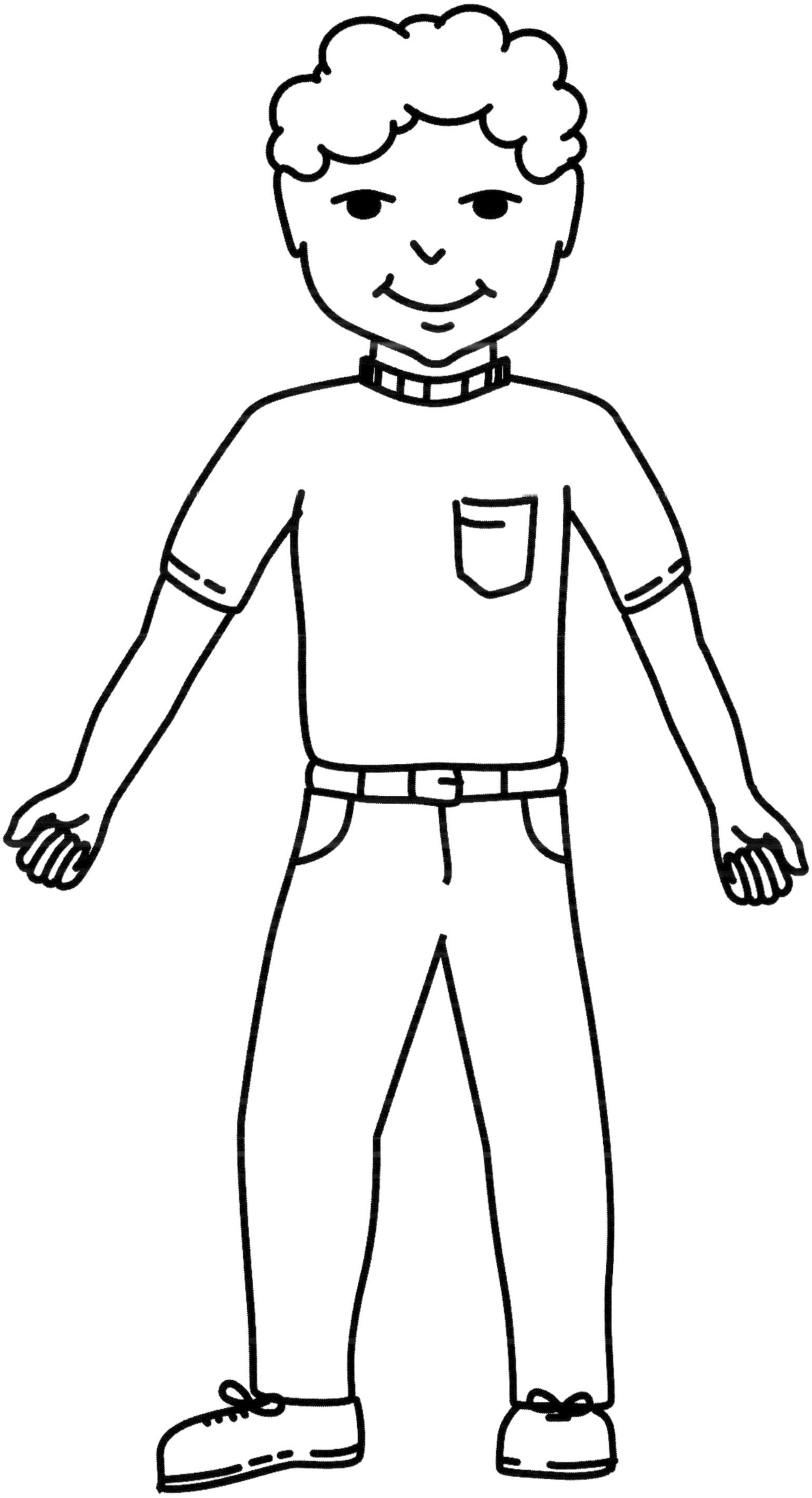

3. I Know My Father Lives

Children's Songbook, 5

Opening Song: "The First Article of Faith," *Children's Songbook,* 122

Closing Song: "I Know My Father Lives," *Children's Songbook,* 5

Materials Needed

- Chalkboard and chalk
- Bible
- Copy of the first article of faith

Preparation

- Prayerfully review the mission and purposes of the Godhead and the Holy Ghost in the Bible Dictionary.

Teaching Suggestions

Begin by asking the children to tell you what the Godhead is. Can they name its members for you? List the members of the Godhead on the board then have the children repeat the first article of faith with you. Explain that each member of the Godhead has a unique purpose; help them determine what each person in the Godhead is supposed to do. Write the main points about each member on the board.

- Heavenly Father is the literal father of our spirits. He created a plan for His children that would help us learn and grow to be like Him.
- Jesus Christ is the literal son of God. He helped create the earth, gave us the example of His life, and atoned for our sins and was resurrected so that we could return to live with Heavenly Father again.
- The Holy Ghost is the testifier. He teaches us the things that are good and true. We feel his presence when we are choosing the right or learning about the gospel. He tells us that we really do have a Heavenly Father who loves us and that Jesus is our Savior. We gain our testimonies by understanding the promptings of the Holy Ghost.

Tell the children that today they will be learning more about the Holy Ghost and one important thing he does. Have the children repeat the things you discussed about the Holy Ghost's mission.

Erase your lists of notations about the Godhead and write the second sentences of both the first and second verses on the board. Leave a larger clear space at the top of the board. Line up the words so that matching words are over top of each other.

Read the first line you wrote to the children and ask if this matches the things you talked about that the Holy Ghost can do. Allow them to name the truths of which he might bear witness of. Ask them how the song says the Holy Ghost will tell them that something is true. (He whispers).

Have them try the following exercise. Time them for at least thirty seconds to see how quiet they can be. Have them sit as quietly as they can and carefully listen to see what they can hear going on around them. When the time is up, commend them for the amount of quiet they were able to achieve and then ask them to share some of the things they heard with you. You might want to make a list on the bottom of the board.

Tell them that this is the same way we can hear the Holy Ghost whispering to us. We must take time to listen, and we must want to hear and be trying our best to be good. When we learn to do this, He can speak to us.

He speaks to us in many different ways, just as the children heard many different things when they were listening. Sometimes it is a quiet voice; sometimes it is just the way we feel. We can feel warm, happy, or peaceful if something is good, or we can feel nervous, upset, or even sick if something is bad. Sometimes when we're listening, someone else will say something that makes us feel good. That is the Holy Ghost speaking to us too. Sometimes our own thoughts just become clearer or make better sense because He is helping us to understand something. The more we listen and try to do what's right, the easier it is to hear what He is trying to tell us.

Repeat the first line from the chalkboard again and have the children say it with you. Then let them hear this part played on the piano. Help them see that there is a movement to the melody line by quietly singing along and using pitch conducting (see "How To Conduct A Song," *Children's Songbook*, 300) Invite them to try singing this line with you while you show them the pitch of the notes.

Next have them slowly sing the line one more time, while you draw out the pitch level on the board. Start at the first word and draw a line above the words that shows if they sing higher or lower in relation to the last note they sang.

Tell the children that they are going to pretend they are the Holy Ghost and that they are trying to whisper something to someone. Can they whisper this line of the song? Have them try it. Then let them try whispering louder and softer following the same line as the pitch. If they are singing higher, they sing louder, if they are singing notes that go down they should try to see if they can sing a little softer for each one. Can they do it?

Next, tell the children that the name of this song is "I Know My Father Lives." Do they remember the things you discussed about Heavenly Father? Remind them once again that we are all His children and He made a plan for us to return to Him. These two things are what the Spirit whispers to us in this song. Tell them the first line of the first verse and have them repeat it with you. Introduce the music and have them sing this line in an even, clear voice. Then add the second line and let them again whisper in coordination with the pitch.

Then introduce the first part of the second verse; repeat it with the children then add the music for normal singing. Show them that the second part of this verse is almost like the first verse. What is the difference? ("[He] tells me that I can.")

Remind the children that Heavenly Father has provided a lot of help for us to help us know that we can live His plan. Ask the children to name some of the things they have discussed today and in previous weeks that Heavenly Father has given us to help us. This list should include the scriptures, parts of the gospel, and, most importantly, the Savior.

Next, have the children first whisper these words and then vary the volume with the notes as they did on the first verse. Have them sing the entire verse.

Ask the children to repeat back to you what the two things are that the song teaches. ("I know my Father lives, and loves me too." And "He sent me here to earth, by faith to live his plan.")

Then ask them what the two things are that the Spirit whispers. ("It is true" and "That I can.")

Add your own testimony of the truthfulness of these two fundamental principles. Be mindful of the presence of the Spirit and share what you feel with them to help them better recognize its presence as well. Then have the children sing the full song one more time with the dynamics in place.

Special note: This song can be learned in two parts. The version in the hymnbook (*Hymns,* no. 302) is written so that the accompaniment plays the melody. The version in the *Children's Songbook* does not play the melody but has a beautiful backdrop with its own melody. It is easiest to teach the melody from the *Hymns*. The next step would be to have a separate recording of just the melody, or a second person on the piano playing the melody an octave higher, while the pianist plays the accompaniment from the *Children's Songbook.*

The goal is to have the children able to sing the melody without following an accompaniment. During the sacrament program, a violin, flute, or organ may be used to provide a supplement of the melody while the children sing and the pianist plays the accompaniment from the *Children's Songbook.*

4. CHOOSING HAPPINESS

Opening Song: "I Need My Heavenly Father," *Children's Songbook*, 18

Closing Song: "I Will Follow God's Plan for Me," *Children's Songbook*, 164

MATERIALS NEEDED

- Two copies of each included illustration and song title on card stock
- Tape or other fastener
- Chalkboard or other large display area

PREPARATION

- Color, cut, and laminate illustrations and song titles for durability.
- Tape illustrations and songs, randomly, face down in a five-by-six grid.

TEACHING SUGGESTIONS

Explain that before we came to this earth we made a choice to follow Heavenly Father's plan. This plan is sometimes called the plan of happiness because Heavenly Father truly wants us each to be happy. Have the children briefly highlight what they remember about Heavenly Father's plan and our part in it.

Heavenly Father gave us the gift of agency on this earth so that we could continue to make choices. He provided us with guidance, such as the commandments, to help us make choices that would help bring us great happiness. He also provided a Savior to help us make up for those times when we wouldn't choose wisely.

Today, the children will help you identify some of the things we have been given that will help us to be happy and to get back to our Heavenly Father. The children will be given opportunities to make choices to see what some of these things are and sing "happy" songs.

Play a memory game. Pictures match with pictures, and songs match with songs. Children are called up to choose two cards at a time. If the two cards chosen do not match, turn them back over. When a match is made, leave the cards turned over, and discuss how the item pictured brings us happiness and shows we are following Heavenly Father's Plan.

Sing the songs as they are matched up.

End with your testimony of the happiness that the gospel has brought into your life and gratitude for the gift of agency.

PICTURES

- **Baby**—We came to earth to get a body, to be tested, and to make choices that would help us learn how to be more like our Heavenly Father.
- **Family**—Heavenly Father placed us in families so that we could learn and grow together. This was part of Heavenly Father's plan for us.
- **Temple**—We go to the temple to learn more about Heavenly Father and His plan. We make promises to Heavenly Father to do those things that will make us happy and help us return to Him. We can be sealed to our families so that we can always be together.
- **Baptism**—We can be washed clean of all our sins and promise Heavenly Father that we will try to be like His son, Jesus Christ. When we are baptized, we become members of Heavenly Father's church and show Him that it is important to us to continue to learn about Him.
- **Word of Wisdom**—When we follow the word of wisdom, we keep our bodies healthy and clean. This lets us run and play and feel better everyday. When our bodies are clean on the inside and out, we are showing Heavenly Father that we respect the gift of our bodies.
- **Sacrament**—Every week when we take the sacrament, we can remember the covenants that we made when we were baptized. We think about Jesus Christ and all that He has done for us so that we could repent and remain spiritually clean. We make promises to try our best every day to choose the right and to fix things that we have done wrong.
- **Commandments**—Heavenly Father teaches us how to live the Gospel. He gives us rules that help us stay safe and understand Him better. We learn to be more like Heavenly Father when we keep His commandments.
- **Jesus Christ**—Heavenly Father knew that we would make mistakes sometimes, even when we were trying our best. He sent Jesus Christ to live on the earth. He shared His example of how to try our best to keep the commandments and serve Heavenly Father. He also atoned for all of our sins. If we repent, He paid the price for our mistakes and promises to wash them away. He made it possible for us to return to our Heavenly Father.

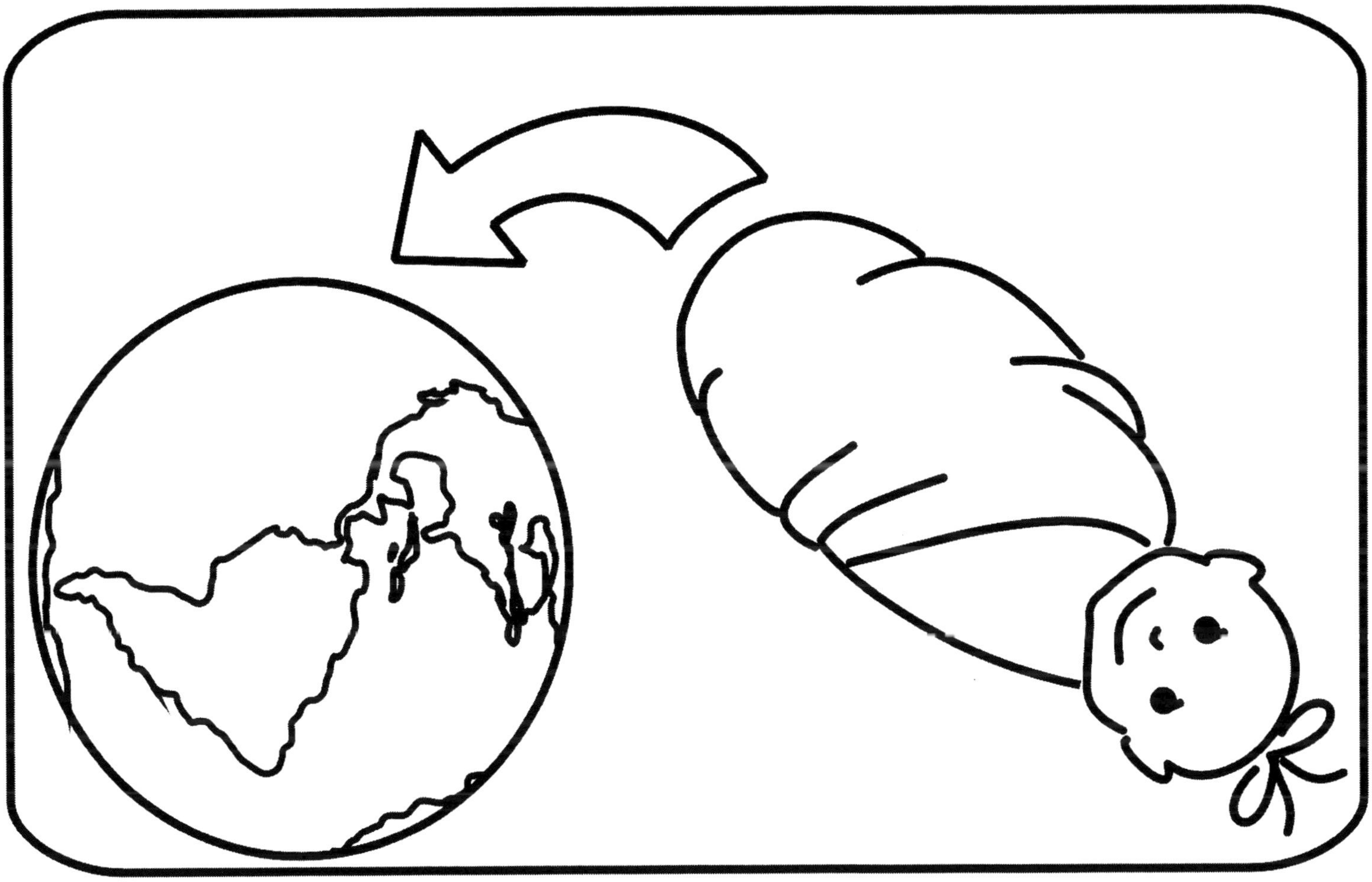

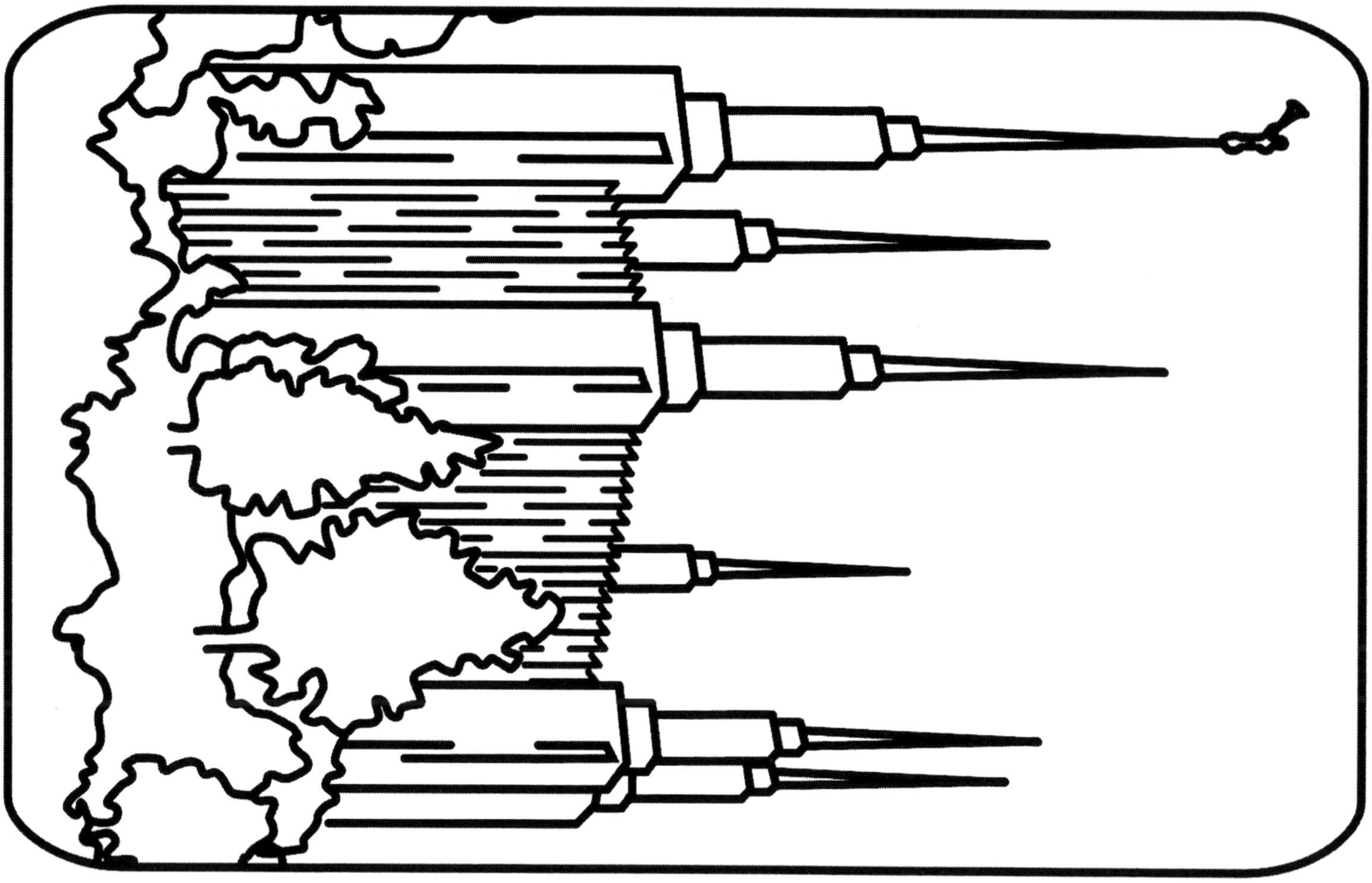

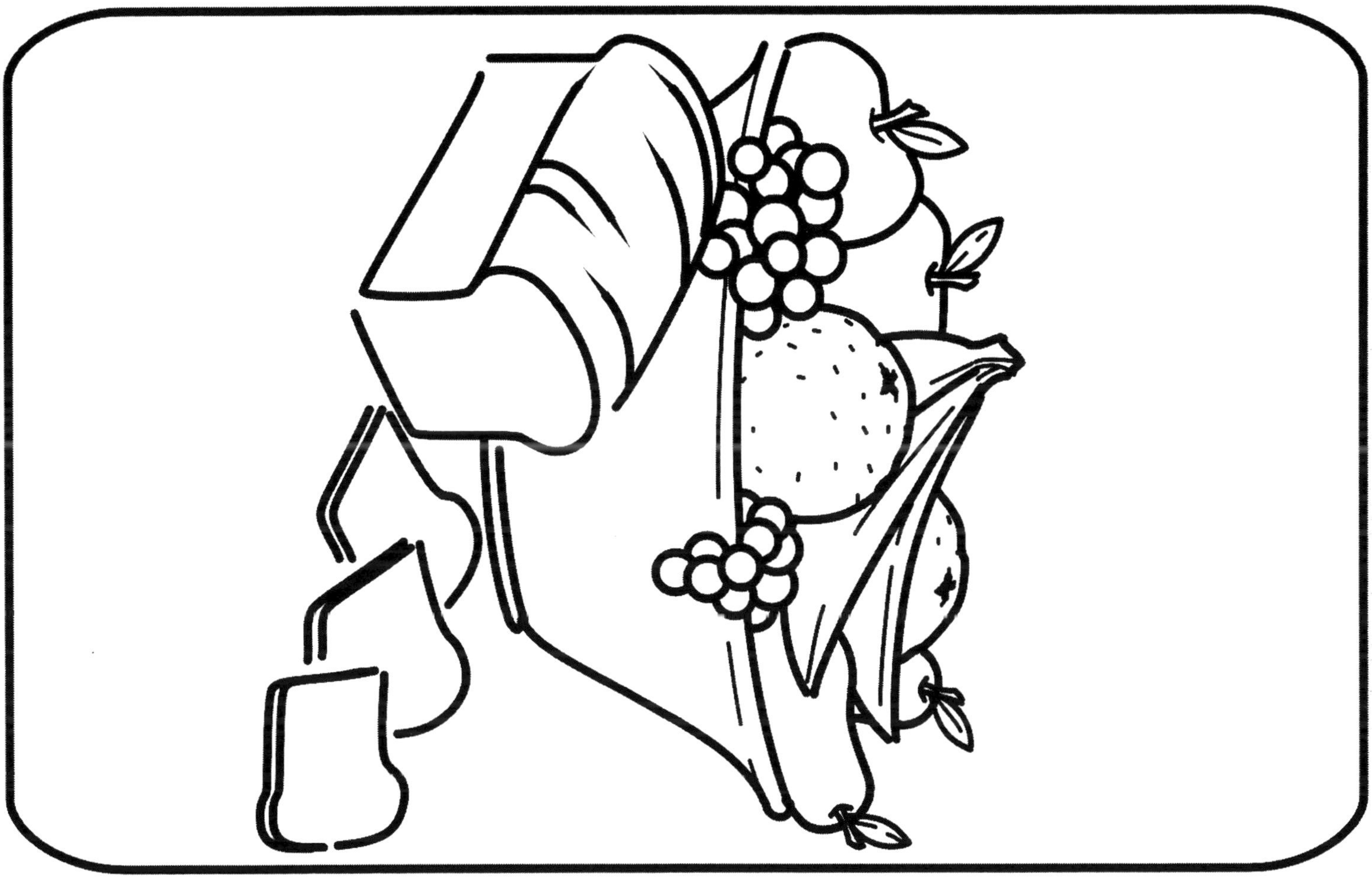

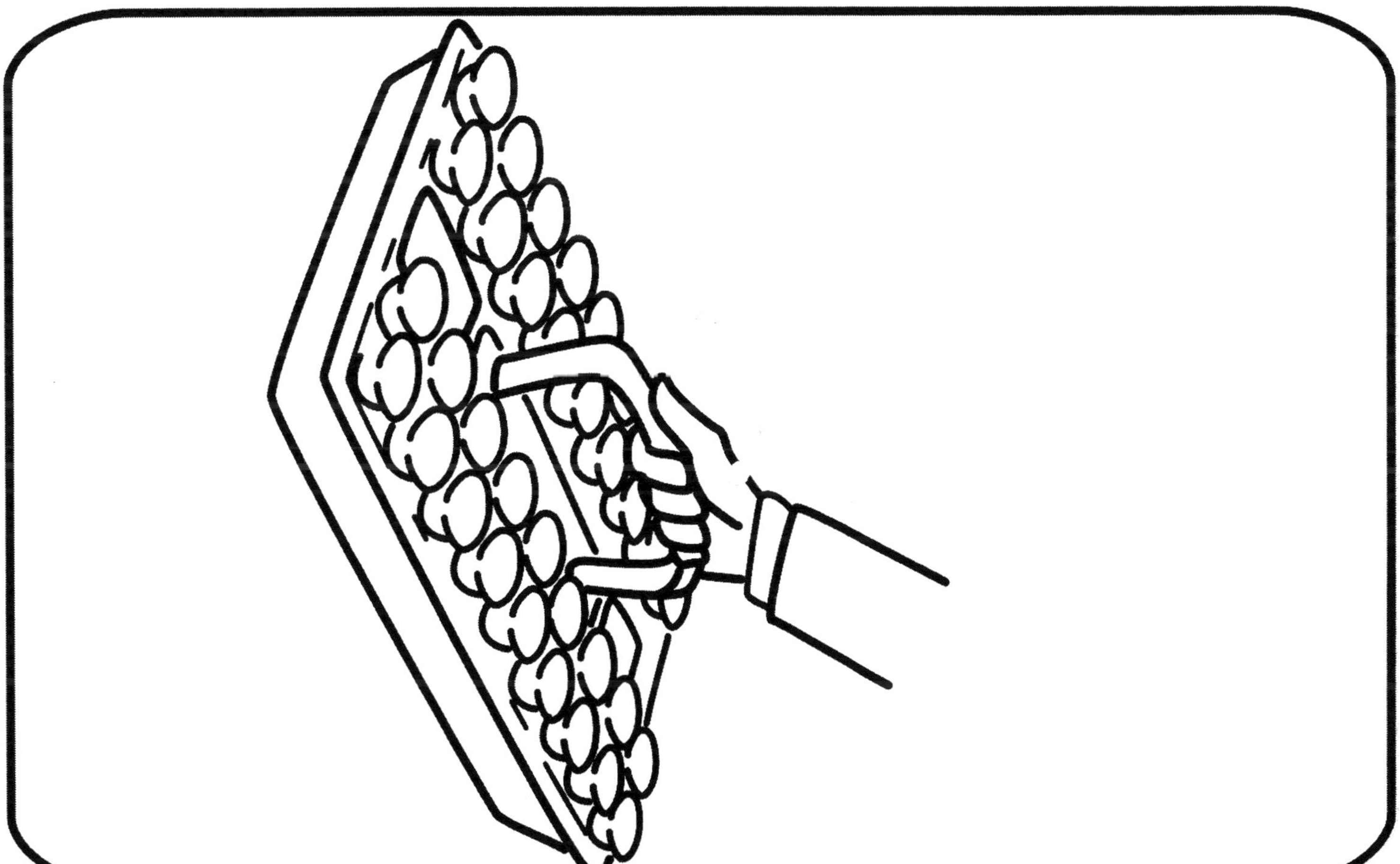

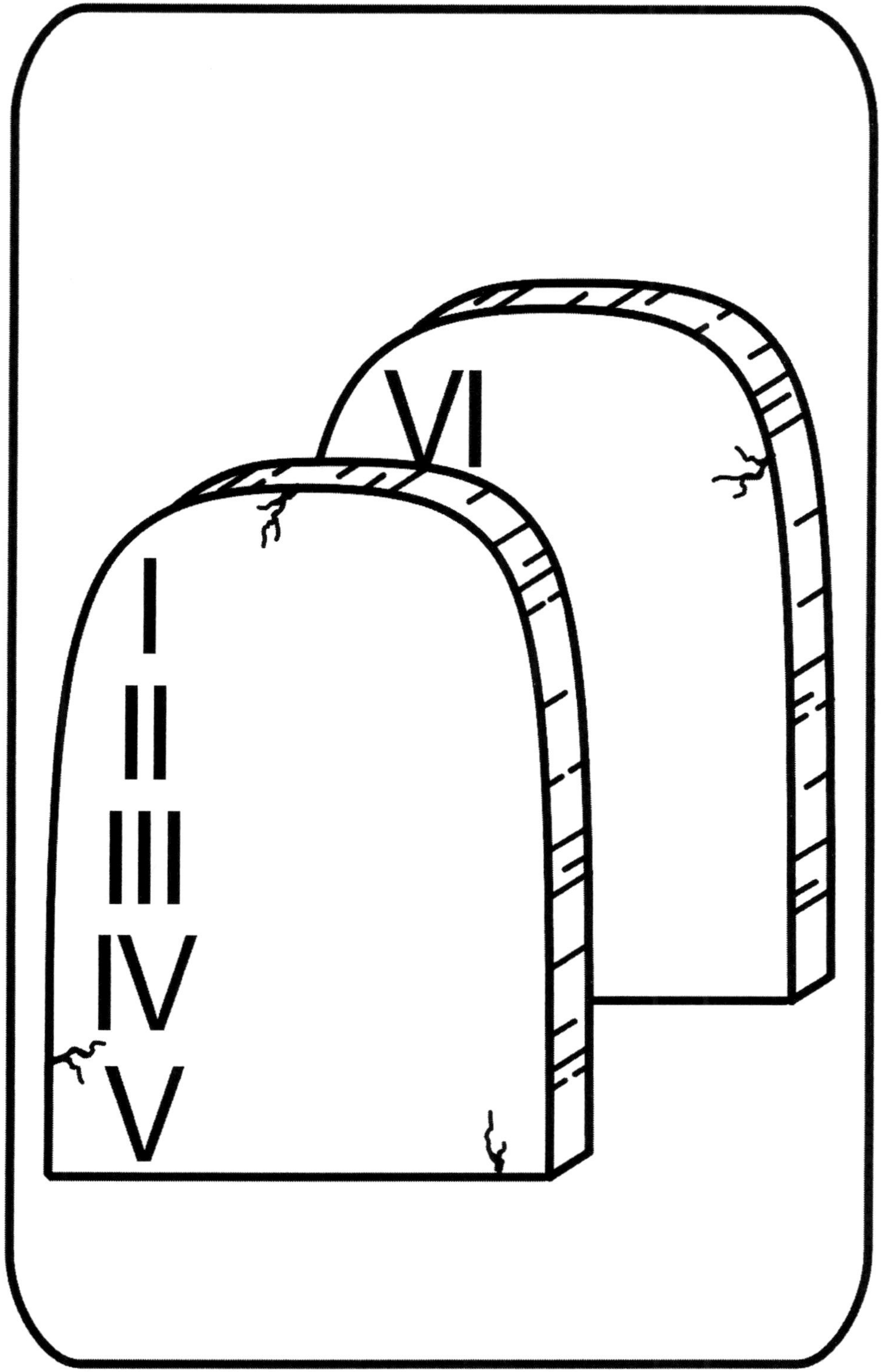
I
II
III
IV
V
VI

Choose the Right Way

160

If You're Happy

266

Happy
Song

264

Jesus
Wants
Me
for a
Sunbeam

60

Smiles

267

I Know My Father Lives

5

Scripture
Power

5. FOLLOW THE PROPHETS

Children's Songbook, 110

Opening Song: "I Want to Live the Gospel," *Children's Songbook*, 148

Closing Song: "Follow the Prophets," *Children's Songbook*, 110

MATERIALS NEEDED

- Gospel Art Pictures # 101, 102, 105, 107, 111, 117, 120
- Primary 6-46 illustration
- Craft sticks or cards, numbered 1–8

PREPARATION

Special Note: All of the verses can be taught by having a special Primary activity day prior to this Sunday sharing time. Teach the rhythm of the song by having the children clap along and learn to chant the last verse. Tell them that they will learn different stories that will follow this same pattern. Set up twenty-minute stations where the children will view the appropriate gospel art picture, learn the story portrayed in each verse and perform a simple activity. At the end of the activity they will learn to chant and clap the words to the corresponding verse of "Follow the Prophets." Each verse will be passed off and a sticker reward given for participating in each group and learning the words.

The following activities may be considered:

- **Adam**—planting seeds or small flowers
- **Enoch**—building graham cracker houses (cities)
- **Noah**—water balloon toss
- **Abraham**—cut and color family trees
- **Moses**—compass course or simple treasure hunt
- **Samuel**—decorate name plates with the children's names
- **Jonah**—fish pond
- **Daniel**—lion craft of some sort (paper bag puppets, decorate sugar cookies with frosting, etc.)

If you do not plan to introduce the words to this song prior to sharing time, assign each class a verse, one through eight, to learn for presentation several weeks in advance.

TEACHING SUGGESTIONS

- If you have held an activity day to introduce this song, present the gospel art pictures used in the activity beginning with verse one and continuing in order. Have the children help you retell the important parts of the story. Chant the verse together, and then let the children hear the melody. Help the children sing and clap along with the piano.

Continue this course until all the verses are covered. Once the melody has been introduced, you don't need to have the piano play it separately each time, just let the children sing along after they have reviewed the words they learned.

- If you do not plan to introduce the words to this song prior to sharing time, assign each class a verse, one through eight, to learn for presentation several weeks in advance. Provide them with the appropriate gospel art picture. Have the children come to the front, tell about their prophet's story, and then sing the verse for the rest of the children. All of the children may sing along with the chorus.

If you are presenting this lesson as a joint sharing time, each class needs to be able to present in a five minute time frame. If you are holding separate sharing times: the classes will have ten minutes to present.

For smaller primaries, prayerfully choose the verses that will leave the greatest gospel message with the children and only present those.

- For either method, close by presenting the ninth verse as a promise to the children that if they follow the prophets, both old and new, they will always know how to choose the right.

Special Note: When using this song at future points in time, provide items (such as craft sticks or cards) that are numbered 1–8. These can be drawn out by reverent children to decide which verses are to be sung that day. Keep the used sticks separate until all verses have been reviewed. Always end with verse nine.

This song can be presented in the Sacrament program by class. Have each class sing one verse (the verse they were responsible for learning if you chose this method) and all the children sing the chorus.

6. Meet the Prophets and Apostles

Opening Song: "The Sixth Article of Faith," *Children's Songbook*, 126

Closing Song: "Follow the Prophets," *Children's Songbook*, 110

Materials Needed

- *Ensign*, November 2005
- Scissors
- Tape or other fasteners
- Construction paper
- Marker
- Chalkboard or other display area
- Small bulk star stickers for each child
- Copies of the Church leaders information from this lesson for each child
- Hymn book
- Large world map

Preparation

- Copy the picture of each prophet and apostle from their individual talks in the *Ensign* and enlarge to approximately a half page size.
- Mount each picture on a piece of construction paper.
- Cut fifteen strips of construction paper, write the bolded words from each General Authorities information sheet on the strips.
- Display the pictures in order on the chalkboard.
- Place the word strips to one side in random order.
- Copy the full sheet from the *Ensign* containing the First Presidency and Quorum of the Twelve Apostles for each child.
- Prepare to have the pianist quietly play "My Redeemer Lives," *Hymns* no. 135 while someone reads the words. This is a short song; the children might even try singing the first verse one time through.
- It would be helpful to find Czechoslovakia to show the children where this is in relation to where they live.

TEACHING SUGGESTIONS

Ask the children if they know whose pictures are displayed. The men shown are our current prophet, his counselors, and the Quorum of the Twelve Apostles. These are the men who speak for Heavenly Father today. They teach us exactly what Heavenly Father wants us to know right now. That is why it is important to listen to the speakers at general conference.

Help the children understand your own love for, and testimony of, our living prophet and the other church leaders. Express to the children that you would like them to get to know these men better. They will learn a little bit about each person shown and learn who they are.

Begin by naming each person in order, and then ask the children to join you in saying their names.

Next show the strips of construction paper you prepared. Tell the children that there is one paper for each man shown. Each paper tells something special about that person.

Begin with President Hinckley. Point to his picture and ask the children to tell you his name. Share the special fact about him, let the children hear the hymn, and then ask a reverent child to come up to find and place the correct word strip under President Hinckley's picture.

Continue by naming each individual, telling about him, and placing the word strip describing him under his picture. Stop after every few names and return to the beginning. Have the children help you repeat the person's name and what they learned about him from the word strip.

When all the word strips have been placed and reviewed, remove half of the strips. Place them at the bottom of the chalkboard.

Call reverent children forward to choose a word strip and try to place it with the correct person. If a match is made, that child may choose their favorite song to sing. If the match is incorrect, the word strip is returned to the bottom. Hints may be given as needed.

Continue until all the word strips have been replaced. Run through the whole list of leaders and their information one more time. Then remind the children of your testimony.

Pass out a copy of the church leader's pictures, information, and fifteen to twenty stars to each child. Encourage them to share what they learned about the prophets and apostles with their family. Tell the children to take their pictures and stars to General Conference with them. They can place a star by the picture of each church leader that they hear speak.

Meet the Prophets and Apostles

Gordon B. Hinckley
Wrote the words to **My Redeemer Lives** (*Hymns, no.* 135).

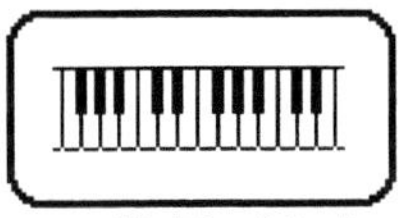

Russell M. Nelson
Loves to sing and play the **piano and organ.**

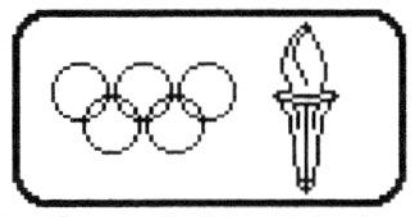

Robert D. Hales
Carried the **Olympic Torch** in 2002.

Thomas S. Monson
Once received a **pet canary** named "**Billie**" as a gift.

Dallin H. Oaks
Loves to **read.**

Jeffrey R. Holland
Loves sports. He played football, basketball, baseball, and track.

James E. Faust
As a child loved the story **"The Little Engine that Could"**

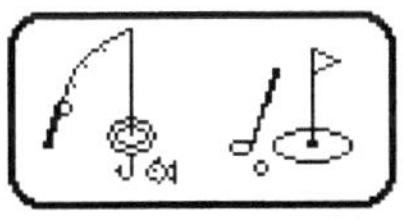

M. Russell Ballard
Likes to **fish and golf.**

Henry B. Eyring
Enjoys **cooking.**

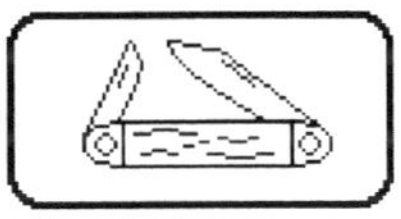

Boyd K. Packer
Makes beautiful **wood carvings.**

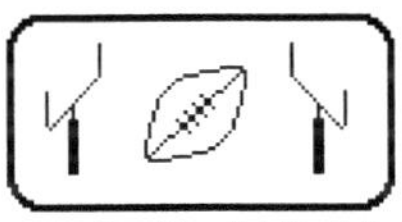

Joseph B. Wirthlin
Played on his **college football** team.

Dieter F. Uchtdorf
Was born in **Czechoslovakia.**

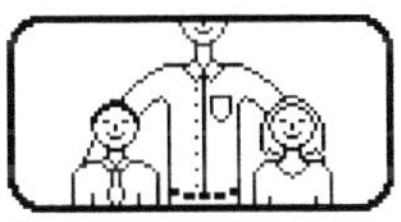

L. Tom Perry
His boyhood nickname was **"stretch"** because he was so tall.

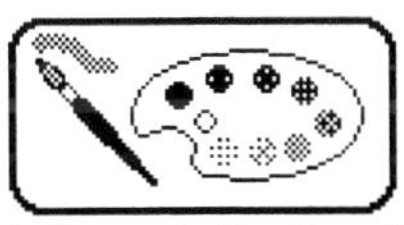

Richard G. Scott
His hobby is **painting.**

David A. Bednar
Was president of **BYU-Idaho** before being called as an apostle.

Note: The information for the above individuals was obtained through various articles in the *Friend* magazine.

7. Did Jesus Really Live Again?

Children's Songbook, 64

Opening Song: "He Sent His Son," *Children's Songbook*, 34

Closing Song: "Did Jesus Really Live Again?" *Children's Songbook*, 64

Materials Needed

- Chalkboard, chalk, and eraser
- Gospel Art Picture #233, 234
- Local newspaper or copy of the Church News if available—choose one with a front page headline that is positive, not discouraging or contrary to the Spirit
- Scriptures

Preparation

- Be familiar with the story of the resurrection found in Matthew 28, Mark 16, Luke 24, and John 20.

Teaching Suggestions

Show the children your newspaper. Ask them why people read newspapers. Newspapers provide us with information about things that are happening—sometimes close to us, sometimes all over the world. People read newspapers because they want to find out what is happening and learn new things. Newspapers answer certain questions about how and when things have happened.

Show the children your scriptures. Ask them why people read the scriptures. Scriptures provide us with the same types of information that a newspaper can, but the stories in the scriptures are told because Heavenly Father knows that learning about them can help us be better people and be happier.

Point out the headline on your newspaper. This title tells you what the story is going to be about. Tell the children that the song they are going to learn today is like a newspaper article—it tells about a special event from the scriptures.

Write the title of the song, "Did Jesus Really Live Again?" across the top of the chalkboard. This is your news headline. Ask the children who they can think of that would be able to answer this question. Allow them to share their answers.

Show the two gospel art pictures, and tell the children that the people from the pictures were some of the first people who could answer the question from the board. Identify Mary and the Apostles and then put the picture of the apostles aside.

Have the children help you tell the story of Mary and the garden tomb. Using the scriptures and the back of the gospel art picture to help, remind the children of all the particular points that will be covered in the first verse of the song.

Next tell the children that they will begin writing their story. Rewrite "Did Jesus really live again?" below the title on the board. Help the children understand that this is the first line of their story and that the story of Mary gives the answers to this question.

Help them sing this line.

To help them know what they should say next, they need to remember Mary's story. Ask pointed questions that will lead to the next phrases, such as How many days did Mary wait before going to the tomb? Was Jesus in the tomb when Mary got there? How did Mary know that it was Jesus whom she saw alive in the garden? As the children give the answers to each question, write that line of the song below the others. At the end of the verse help the children sing the verse through several times before moving on.

Follow this same pattern with verses two and three, the information for these verses is all contained in the story of Jesus' time with the disciples. Review this story, including the important information they will need to answer your questions and gain each new song phrase.

When all three verses have been listed, and reviewed, have the children sing the entire song. Be mindful of the presence of the Spirit. Help the children understand how the Spirit works to testify to them that the things they have learned today are true. The Holy Ghost promises that we will all live again because of what Jesus did for us.

If there is time remaining, go back through your questions and erase the key word answer from each phrase. Then challenge the children to use what they have learned today to fill in the missing words as they sing. Commend their efforts and knowledge of the resurrection.

8. SEEKING REPENTANCE

Opening Song: "Repentance," *Children's Songbook*, 98

Closing Song: "Help Me, Dear Father," *Children's Songbook*, 99

MATERIALS NEEDED

- One copy of the word search on a transparency sheet for overhead projector
- Dry-erase marker
- Copies of the word search for every child
- Pencils for each child
- Overhead projector

PREPARATION

- Place the overhead projector in a position that allows for visibility by all the children.

TEACHING SUGGESTIONS

Talk about the steps of repentance and its importance. Tell the children that when we first come to earth, we are clean and pure. But as we learn and grow, sometimes we make choices that don't leave us clean. We can sin. A sin is anything that makes us less clean and less like our Heavenly Father. These sins can be things everyone can see or things that only our Heavenly Father can see.

Ask the children what they think it would take to become clean again after we sin. Allow them to share their ideas.

Explain to the children that we have been given the gift of repentance When we do something wrong, we need to go through a certain process to make it right. First, we recognize that we have done something wrong. Then we talk to our Heavenly Father and sometimes our Bishop about it. They can help us know what we need to do to make things right. We also promise to try and never do it again. When we do these things, the Savior can finish the process for us. Jesus Christ atoned for our sins so that we could repent.He has promised that if we truly repent, He will take away every bit of that sin. He will make us clean and pure again.

When we are baptized and when we take the sacrament, we are making a covenant, or promise, with Heavenly Father and Jesus that we want to be clean and pure. We promise to try our best to do what is right and to repent when we do things that are wrong. When we do this, they promise to always forgive us and help us as we try to do better.

Introduce the word search. Tell the children that this puzzle contains words that will help them understand more about repentance. Allow the senior Primary some time to see how many words they can find on their own. With the junior Primary, go straight to the overhead projector and help them find each word.

With both groups: use the overhead projector and transparency to show the children where each word is located. When a word is circled, go over what the term means and read the accompanying scripture or sing the song before moving to the next term. End with your testimony of the importance of repentance.

WORD LIST

- **Accountability**—The second article of faith
- **Agency**—2 Nephi 2:27
- **Atonement**—"To Think About Jesus," *Children's Songbook*, 71
- **Blessing**—Malachi 3:10
- **Consequence**—2 Corinthians 5:10
- **Covenant**—Deuteronomy 29:12
- **Holy Ghost**—"The Holy Ghost," *Children's Songbook*, 105
- **Plan**—"I Lived in Heaven," *Children's Songbook*, 4
- **Repent**—Mosiah 26:30
- **Resurrection**—"Did Jesus Really Live Again?" *Children's Songbook*, 64
- **Savior**—"He Sent His Son," *Children's Songbook*, 34
- **Sin**—2 Peter 2:21

Repentance Word Search

		O	P	E	N	T	I	B	E	A	R		
	T	B	R	I	S	A	V	I	O	R	E	P	
S	O	E	O	D	E	T	I	S	A	Y	S	O	F
A	R	A	P	W	B	O	P	H	C	I	U	P	M
C	D	G	H	O	L	N	L	O	H	V	R	R	Z
O	I	E	E	X	E	E	A	P	A	T	R	E	A
V	N	N	T	O	S	M	Y	S	P	I	E	P	H
E	A	C	O	N	S	E	Q	U	E	N	C	E	B
N	N	Y	K	S	I	N	E	B	L	E	T	N	U
A	C	C	O	U	N	T	A	B	I	L	I	T	Y
N	E	H	P	M	G	E	I	E	I	O	O	C	S
T	H	O	L	Y	G	H	O	S	T	I	N	G	A
	N	S	A	V	C	H	U	R	C	H	S	W	
		T	N	E	M	N	O	T	A	M	Y		

Word List

Accountability	Holy Ghost
Agency	Plan
Atonement	Repent
Blessing	Resurrection
Consequence	Savior
Covenant	Sin

9. HOLDING HANDS AROUND THE WORLD

Friend, July 2002, 44-45

Opening Song: "We'll Bring the World His Truth," *Children's Songbook*, 172

Closing Song: "Holding Hands Around the World," *Friend*, July 2002, 44-45

MATERIALS NEEDED

- One poster board
- Tape, glue, or other adhesive

PREPARATION

- Illustrations are presented in the order of use. They can be enlarged and placed on a poster board to use as reference. Please note that all words are not included. Sign language does not share the same grammar as English, so not all of the words are signed.
- Become familiar with the included sign language gestures for this song. Do not be as concerned with signing each word as it is sung; emphasize a smooth flow from one sign to the next. Each sign can be used as clues to a phrase, not necessarily that specific word.

TEACHING SUGGESTIONS

Introduce this song by its title. Talk with the children about the many different ways we can use our hands to help others. Ask them what they think the title of this song could mean and allow them to share their responses.

Tell the children that even though Heavenly Father's children live in all different places, have different appearances, traditions, and lives, every child deserves to know that Heavenly Father loves them. When we share the gospel with others, we are passing a great gift around the world: the gift of Heavenly Father's love. This gift joins everyone around the world together. Ask the children to name some specific ways they can help share this gift with others.

Express to the children that their actions and their words are a great testimony to others. Encourage them to remember to show the goodness of the gospel in everything that they do. Tell them they will learn how to sing this song with their mouths and their hands to help them remember to be righteous.

Recite the chorus to the children, while you sign the key words. Have them repeat each word back to you and mimic the accompanying sign. After they have some confidence in the signs, let them hear what the piano plays as you sign and sing along. Let the children then try to sing the chorus while creating the motions. Commend them for their efforts.

Next read the first phrase of the first verse. Ask the children if they heard any words used that they already know how to sign (children and world). Introduce the melody and have the children try to sing along and add the signs they know. Repeat the first phrase again for the children and show them the additional signs they can use. Sing the phrase again with all the signs in place.

Add the next phrase and its signs and then try signing it as well. Frequently review the previous phrases by having reverent children or other leaders come to the front to help you sign and direct the song to the point learned.

As you teach the words and signs, share your testimony and appreciation for the message and commend the children often for their efforts.

This is a longer song and seems a little daunting to learn in this manner, but children usually love this experience and won't mind the length because they are able to move and actively participate in their learning. It also helps that this is an upbeat song. If you show enthusiasm for the message and the children's efforts, your happiness will be contagious!

Special Note: While the children are first learning, have the pianist play at a slower rate than suggested on the music. As they become more proficient and enthusiastic, the tempo can be gradually increased.

"Holding Hands Around The World"
Sign Language: Chorus

"Holding Hands Around The World"
Sign Language: 1st Verse - Part 1

"Holding Hands Around The World"
Sign Language: 1st Verse - Part 2

"Holding Hands Around The World"
Sign Language: 2nd Verse - Part 1

"Holding Hands Around The World"
Sign Language: 2nd Verse - Part 2

10. The Things Jesus Taught

Opening Song: "I Think When I Read That Sweet Story," *Children's Songbook*, 56

Closing Song: "I'm Trying to Be Like Jesus," *Children's Songbook*, 78

Materials Needed

- Gospel Art Pictures #211, 218, 219, 221, 225, 226, 234, 235, 323 (all pictures will not be used; if you want to limit the options, prayerfully consider which messages are most important for your Primary to focus on)
- Children's Songbooks for children to use
- Strips of construction paper
- Pens or markers for use by children/leaders
- Tape or other fasteners

Preparation

- Be familiar with the gospel stories portrayed in the pictures and the basic gospel lesson they portray so that you are able to assist the classes as needed.

Teaching Suggestions

Let each class choose a gospel art picture, a strip of construction paper, and marking pen. Provide copies of the Children's Songbook for referencing.

Have the teacher discuss with the children what story their picture is trying to tell and review its main points. Ask the classes to decide what message Jesus Christ wanted us to learn from this story. Have the teacher write that principle on the strip of paper. Classes may come up with more than one idea; have other strips available if they are needed. Next, ask the classes to find a Primary song that they think talks about their gospel lesson.

Each class will come up to the front, show their picture, briefly tell the story, post their word strip, and announce their chosen song for the Primary to sing. Sing the song before moving to the next class.

When all the classes have presented their message, ask the children what they think the most important thing they learned today would be. Allow them to share their answers. Assure them that their answers are all correct, but the most important lesson is to always look to Jesus Christ for any answer. Learning to know and trust His teachings is the most important thing anyone can do.

Testify of your gratitude for the Savior's life and example. Share with the children that if they will always try to learn about and be more like Jesus Christ, they will always know what is right.

11. Dearest Children, God Is Near You

Hymns, no. 96

Opening Song: "God is Watching Over All," *Children's Songbook*, 229

Closing Song: "Dearest Children, God is Near You," *Hymns,* no. 96

Materials Needed

- Copy of illustrations included with lesson
- Copy of situations from lesson
- Tape
- Scissors

Preparation

- Color each illustration.
- Cut out situations and tape them on the back of the corresponding picture.
- Laminate illustrations if desired.

Teaching Suggestions

This hymn will be introduced by melody first. Allow the children to hear the piano play the song one time through while they sit as quietly as they can. Commend them for how well they are able to sit quietly. Share your feelings about listening to this peaceful melody and ask the children to share theirs as well.

Next, work with the children to learn the melody by humming along with each line until they can hum the entire melody.

Remind them of the peaceful feelings and presence of the Spirit. To learn the words to this song, you will talk to them about three children. As you talk about the child's situation, it will help them remember the message and wording of each verse.

Hold up the picture for the first verse and read the short scenario you placed on the back. Ask the children what they think about Bobby's situation. What are their suggestions for what would help, how does Bobby probably feel, and what do they think Bobby should chose to do?

Assure the children that Heavenly Father is concerned about each of us. He knows what makes us happy, and He knows our fears. Read the first verse to the children while they hum along with the piano. Ask them to tell you what answers they heard in the words to the verse. Repeat the words again and let the children echo you a few times, then try singing the words with the piano.

Continue this pattern with the second and third verses, continually assuring the children that Heavenly Father is aware of them personally and wants to help all of His children be happy.

After all three verses have been discussed, if there is time remaining, go back to the first picture and help the children remember what words they sang, review the second and third verses, then try singing all three verses together.

STORIES

- **Verse 1:** Bobby is woken up by some thunder. He's really scared. The lights have gone out in the house and Bobby is afraid of the dark. On top of that, the thunder is really loud.
- **Verse 2:** Jennifer walked into the bathroom just before Primary. Two of her friends were standing at the sink talking about the strange new girl they'd seen earlier. They were all alone, and Jennifer did think the girl looked a little funny. She felt bad that they were saying unkind things about the girl, but she didn't think it would hurt just to listen.
- **Verse 3:** Joseph loved his new skateboard. He could go faster than ever with it, and he was learning some cool tricks. Joseph was riding his skateboard down the road when he got a funny feeling that he should stop. Joseph didn't want to stop, but now his stomach was getting a little upset.

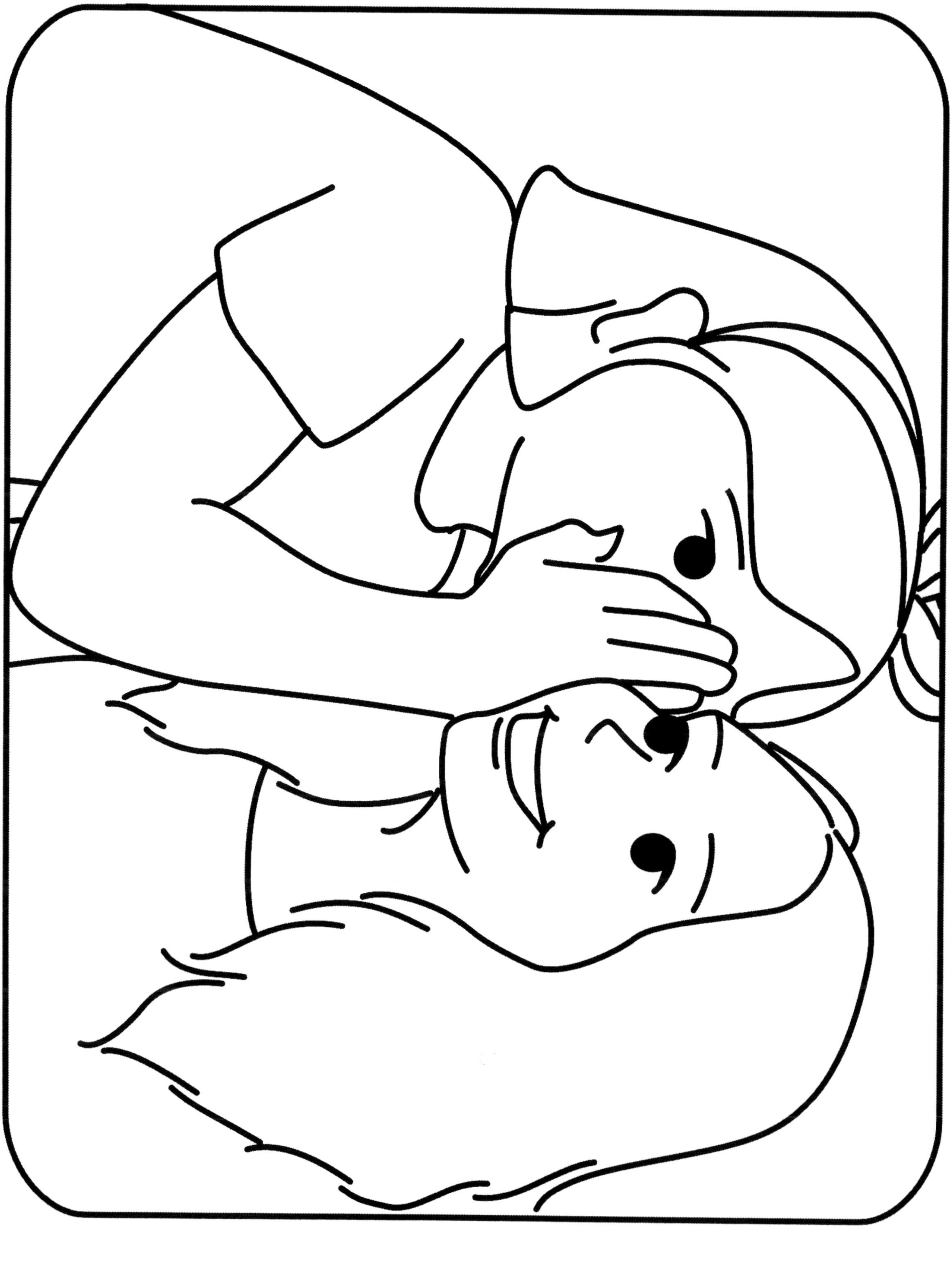

12. NAME THAT GOSPEL STANDARD

Opening Song: "The Commandments," *Children's Songbook*, 112

Closing Song: "I Want to Live the Gospel," *Children's Songbook*, 148

MATERIALS NEEDED

- Chalk and chalkboard
- Large poster of "My Gospel Standards" (expendable)
- Copy of "My Gospel Standards," full page size, for each child
- Gospel Art Picture #107
- Tape or other fastener
- Scissors
- Bag or other container

PREPARATION

- Cut the poster of "My Gospel Standards" into twelve puzzle pieces.
- Place the pieces of the puzzle in a bag or other container to draw from.

TEACHING SUGGESTIONS

Show the children the picture of Moses. Ask them to tell you everything they can remember about this prophet. Commend them for their answers. Tell the children that Moses was given some special instructions from Jehovah, called commandments. These commandments were given to Moses so that he could tell the people exactly what Jehovah wanted them to do and be like.

These same commandments are still very important. Today, we not only have the ten commandments, but we have an additional set of guidelines to help us understand how important those commandments are. These guidelines help us understand what we can do every day to become better, happier people. Ask the children to guess what these guidelines might be. Show a page-size copy of "My Gospel Standards."

You will play the game "name that tune" to help the children identify some of the things that are covered in "My Gospel Standards." Have the piano begin playing one of the songs from this lesson. The first child to reverently raise his or her hand and correctly identify the song being played will choose a puzzle piece from your sack and place it on the board where they think it goes. Lead the children in a discussion of what lesson they think the song teaches them. Reinforce their thoughts by reading to them what "My Gospel Standards" says about this gospel concept. Sing each song before going on to the next one.

When all the songs have been sung, the picture of the gospel standards will be complete. Bare your testimony of the importance of the things they have learned today.

Give each child a copy of "My Gospel Standards" and encourage them to place it somewhere that they will see it every day to remind them of Heavenly Father's commandments and how to live them every day.

PHRASES AND SONGS

1. "I will follow Heavenly Father's plan for me."

    Song: "I Will Follow God's Plan," *Children's Songbook*, 164

2. "I will remember my baptismal covenant and listen to the Holy Ghost."

    Song: "When Jesus Christ was Baptized," *Children's Songbook*, 102

3. "I will choose the right. I know I can repent when I make a mistake."

    Song: "Choose the Right Way," *Children's Songbook*, 160

4. "I will be honest with Heavenly Father, others, and myself."

    Song: "I Believe in Being Honest," *Children's Songbook*, 149

5. "I will use the names of Heavenly Father and Jesus Christ reverently. I will not swear or use crude words."

    Song: "Hum Your Favorite Hymn," *Children's Songbook*, 152

6. "I will do those things on the Sabbath that will help me feel close to Heavenly Father and Jesus Christ."

    Song: "Remember the Sabbath Day," *Children's Songbook*, 155

7. "I will honor my parents and do my part to strengthen my family."

    Song: "Love is Spoken Here," *Children's Songbook*, 190

8. "I will keep my mind and body sacred and pure, and I will not partake of things that are harmful to me."

    Song: "The Lord Gave Me a Temple," *Children's Songbook*,, 153

9. "I will dress modestly to show respect for Heavenly Father and myself."

    Song: "I am a Child of God," *Children's Songbook*, 2

10. "I will only read and watch things that are pleasing to Heavenly Father. I will only listen to music that is pleasing to Heavenly Father."

    Song: "The Thirteenth Article of Faith," *Children's Songbook*, 132

11. "I will seek good friends and treat others kindly."

    Song: "Friends are Fun," *Children's Songbook*, 262

12. "I will live now to be worthy to go to the temple, serve a mission, and do my part to have an eternal family."

    Song: "I Love to See the Temple," *Children's Songbook*, 95

13. Tell Me, Dear Lord

Children's Songbook, 176

Opening Song: "A Child's Prayer," *Children's Songbook*, 12

Closing Song: "Tell Me, Dear Lord," *Children's Songbook*, 176

Materials Needed

- Eight large word Strips
- Chalk and chalkboard
- Tape or other fasteners
- Primary 4–36 illustration
- One sturdy chair that is safe for a child to stand on
- Book of Mormon
- Television and VCR
- Video of The First Vision: *Doctrine and Covenants and Church History* Video Presentations (nine minutes), set to the prayer scene

Preparation

- Write the following words on a word strip: thine (1), thou (2), thy (5).
- Write the words to the song on the board leaving spaces for—but not including—the words that are on your word strips.
- Post the word strips to the side or bottom of the lyrics.
- Review Alma 31:8–23. Pick one or two appropriate verses for a child to read.

Teaching Suggestions

Ask a reverent, older child to come to the front of the room. Have them stand on top of a sturdy chair to read your selected verses from the Zoramites' prayer. Show the children the Primary illustration and briefly review the basic story of the Zoramites and the Rameumptom to help them understand that what was read was meant to be prayer.

Ask the child who read for you what his or her feelings were; let the other children share their feelings about the Zoramites' activities. Help them understand the Zoramites' motivation for saying their prayers in that manner and the misunderstandings they had about whom they were praying to and why.

Next share the video of the first vision. Ask the children to compare the two methods of prayer. How were their feelings different when watching the video from when they were discussing the Zoramites? Ask for their suggestions of when, where, and why it is appropriate to pray.

Explain to the children that we don't need towers for God to hear us, but we do need to understand whom we're talking to and how to talk to Him. When we understand these things, our prayers can bring us closer to Heavenly Father. When we pray because we really do want to talk to Heavenly Father, the Holy Spirit can be there with us. Those special, warm, and good feelings we experience during our most sincere prayers are Heavenly Father's way of letting us know He is listening and loves us very much.

Tell the children that they will learn a song today that will help them remember what prayers should be like.

Demonstrate that there is also a language of reverence that we should use during our prayers. Have the children open their scriptures and find the words that are used as pronouns. This language appears on every page of the scriptures, but Alma 31:26–35 shows Alma's response to the Zoramites' prayer, using these special pronouns. Identify the pronouns used to address Heavenly Father. Point them out on the word strips.

Read through the lyrics to the song. Pause when you come to a break and have the children try to figure out which word should fill the blank.

Introduce the melody as each phrase is completed and have the children try to sing the words to that point as you point out the lyrics on the board. When all the words have been appropriately placed, review the entire song once again.

Challenge the children to remember to use reverent terms when talking to Heavenly Father during their prayers.

14. Mystery Scripture Guests

Opening Song: "A Child's Prayer," *Children's Songbook,* 12

Closing Song: "Tell Me, Dear Lord," *Children's Songbook,* 176

Materials Needed

- Moveable chalkboard or other large barrier
- Gospel Art Picture #107, 305, 402
- Primary 2-34 illustration

Preparation

- Invite various members of your ward to participate in this sharing time, by playing the role of one of the individuals below. He should be familiar with the associated scripture story, emphasizing the importance of prayer, and be prepared to tell the story in three to five minutes, interact with the children, and introduce the appropriate song. Simple costumes are optional but encouraged.
- Arrange the Primary room so that there is an area blocked from the children's view. The individuals playing your guest roles must be able to sit or stand behind the barrier, but they also need access to come out in to the Primary room. Guests should be hidden when the children enter the Primary room.

Teaching Suggestions

Tell the children that they will have several special guests with them in sharing time today. Each person is told about in the scriptures. They have special experiences to share about how prayer has blessed their lives. The guests are shy; the children must first listen to their story without seeing them. If the children can guess who the mystery scripture guest is, he will come out and talk to them.

Have each guest briefly tell their story from behind the barrier. When the children guess correctly, the guest should come out from behind the barrier with the Gospel Art Picture of themselves. The children can ask a couple of questions about that person's experience with prayer. Then the individual should bear a brief testimony of prayer, encourage the children to pray, and ask the children to sing for him.

Continue until all the guests have been revealed.

Guests

- **Daniel**—Daniel 6—"Dearest Children, God is Near You," *Hymns,* no. 96

- **Zacharias**—Luke 1:5–25, 57–80—"Baptism," *Children's Songbook*, 100
- **Enos**—Enos 1—"I Pray in Faith," *Children's Songbook*, 14
- **Joseph Smith**—Joseph Smith–History 1:1–20—"The Sacred Grove," *Children's Songbook*, 87

15. SEARCH, PONDER, AND PRAY

Children's Songbook, 109

Opening Song: "Scripture Power," *Friend,* October 1987, 10–11

Closing Song: "Search, Ponder, and Pray," *Children's Songbook*, 109

MATERIALS NEEDED

- Large paper heart
- Wall calendar
- Gospel Art Picture #402
- One set of scriptures

PREPARATION

- Anticipate hiding places for the items on the materials list.
- Prepare a set of clues for the children to read that will lead them to find the articles that will be used in the song. The scriptures should be the last item found.
- Hide the song prompts in their appropriate places before the children enter the Primary room.

TEACHING SUGGESTIONS

Tell the children that they will help you with a treasure hunt. There are things hidden around the Primary room that they will use in their lesson today. Choose a reverent child to read the first clue and begin the search. As each item is found, let the children express their opinions on how the items could relate to the gospel. Acknowledge their answers; do not provide any further information.

After the scriptures have been found, share your testimony of the value of the scriptures. Ask the children to share some of their favorite stories or thoughts about the scriptures as well.

Remind the children of the important things they have learned about the scriptures this year. Tell them that they will be learning a song that will help them remember how to study the scriptures. Just as you gave them clues and let them search for the items that were needed, Heavenly Father expects us to ask questions and search for the answers in His words.

When we have a question, we should go to the scriptures and search for an answer. When we read, we should also spend time praying about the things we've read. Then the Spirit can help us understand the things we are studying. The Holy Ghost will help us know how those things can help us.

Introduce the words to the song at this time. After teaching the children each phrase, allow them to repeat it back to you while the pianist quietly plays that portion of the song.

After each verse, have reverent children come to the front of the room to help remind everyone of the words to the song they will sing. Have the child hold up their assigned item, or show the actions indicated for the phrases while the words are repeated again. Then let the children sing the verse while the children at the front continue to prompt them for each phrase. Choose new children for the second verse.

Be mindful of the Spirit and reiterate your testimony of the importance of the scriptures. Then close by singing both verses with different children acting as props.

Words and Actions

Verse 1:

- "I love to read the Holy Scriptures, And, ev'ry time I do"—hold up scriptures
- "I feel the Spirit start to grow with in my heart—a testimony that they're true"—hold up heart

Chorus:

- "Search"—hold hand to eyes as if looking for something
- "Ponder"—place finger to side of forehead and pretend to think
- "and pray are the things that I must do"—fold arms, bow head
- "The Spirit will guide, and, deep inside"—point to chest
- "I'll know the scriptures are true"—hold up scriptures again

Verse 2:

- "So, prayerfully I'll read the scriptures"—hold up scriptures
- "Each day my whole life through."—hold up calendar
- "I'll come to understand. I'll heed the Lord's command and live as he would have me do"—hold up Gospel Art Picture

Repeat chorus

16. Building Noah's Ark

Opening Song: "Follow the Prophets," *Children's Songbook*, 110

Closing Song: "I Know My Father Lives," *Children's Songbook*, 5

Materials Needed

- Gospel Art Picture #103
- One and a half paper plates per child
- Green yarn
- Several single hole punches
- Crayons or colored pencils for children to use
- Bulk miniature animal stickers (these can be found inexpensively at most discount stores)
- Scissors

Preparation

- Prepare packages for each teacher ahead of time including: enough full and half piece paper plates for each child, one piece of green yarn (approximately eight to ten inches long) for each child, a hole punch, crayons or colored pencils, and stickers for use by the children.
- Review the story of Noah and the ark found in Genesis 6–9.
- Assemble one mobile ahead of time so you are familiar with its construction.

Teaching Suggestions

Show the gospel art picture and tell the children that today they are going to talk about Noah. Explain that you will help the children make something they can take home with them. This will help remind the children of Noah, how the Lord helped him, and the promises the Lord made to him, and us today. Use the songs to signal the children to finish each portion of the activity and prepare themselves to listen to the next part of the story and the directions.

Story and Construction

"Noah lived a long time ago. When Noah was a prophet, the world was a very bad place to live."

Show a full size paper plate, to represent the earth, and color it black or another dark color. Have the teachers pass out a paper plate to each child and let them color it with a dark color as well.

Sing: "Teach Me to Walk in the Light," *Children's Songbook*, 177

"Heavenly Father was so sad that His children had become wicked that He knew He needed to change things. He wanted to get rid of all the bad things that were happening. So He decided to flood the whole earth. This would clean away all the bad and give the good things a chance to grow again."

"Noah and his family weren't bad, so Heavenly Father told Noah to build a boat for his family. If he built the boat, they would be safe, and they would be able to keep some of the animals safe too."

Fold your paper plate in half so that the dark side you colored is on the inside. The curved portion of the plate is the bottom of the boat; the straight portion is the top. Color one side of the plate so that it resembles a boat. Let the children copy this step.

Sing: "The Wise Man and the Foolish Man," *Children's Songbook*, 281

"When the boat was finished, Heavenly Father told Noah to put his family and two of each kind of animal into the boat. When everyone was inside the ark, Noah sealed the doors and it began to rain"

Draw a stick figure family and place several animal stickers on the other side of the "boat" paper plate. Have the teachers pass out a small number of stickers to each child and let them draw a family and place stickers on the other side of their boats.

Sing: "Rain Is Falling All Around," *Children's Songbook*, 241

"It rained for forty days, till the earth was completely covered in water. Noah's boat kept his family and all the animals safe and dry." Have everyone place their boats on the floor or their seat and gently push them so that they rock on their bottom edge. Count out loud to forty, while you rock your boats.

"When all the earth was covered in water, Noah and his family had to float along for another 150 days. While they waited for the dry land to appear again, Heavenly Father helped and blessed them."

"When the earth began to dry up, Noah's ark stopped on top of a mountain called Ararat. Everyone waited here for a long time to let the rest of the earth to start to dry out and grow things again."

"Noah wondered how he would know it was safe to let his family and all the animals leave the ark. He opened a window on the ark and let out a raven to see if it could find dry land." Use the hole punch to place a hole in the top, middle portion of the ark.

"The raven came back because it couldn't find any place to land. Next, Noah opened the window and let a dove fly out. "

Take the half piece of paper plate and punch a hole in the middle of the straight edge. Ask the teachers to place holes in each child's ark, and then punch holes and pass out the half plates to each child.

Sing: "Popcorn Popping," *Children's Songbook*, 242

"The first time the dove went out, it couldn't find any dry land either. But the next time it flew out, the dove came back with a small twig from an olive tree in its beak."

Show your piece of green yarn. Give each child a piece of yarn to hold.

"The next time Noah let the dove go, it did not come back at all. Noah knew that the dove had found someplace to live. This meant that there was enough dry land to let everyone out of the ark."

"When Noah and his family left the ark, they were very happy to see the beautiful earth again. As they were looking around, they saw something in the sky that made their hearts very happy. It was a rainbow. Heavenly Father told Noah that He made the rainbow to show His promise. Heavenly Father promised Noah that He would never flood the whole earth again."

Hold your half piece of paper plate up so that the curved edge is at the top. Color several stripes of a rainbow on your plate. Then let the children color rainbows on their plates.

Sing: "When I Am Baptized," *Children's Songbook*, 103

Share your testimony with the children of the truths from the song they just sang and your thankfulness for Heavenly Father's promises. Help them be mindful of the Spirit as you share your testimony with them and assure them that feeling the Spirit is another way that Heavenly Father tells us that He will keep his promises to us. Encourage the children to share what they have learned and felt with their families.

Show the children how to tie their rainbows above their arks, joining them with the pieces of green yarn.

Sing: "I Know My Father Lives," *Children's Songbook*, 5

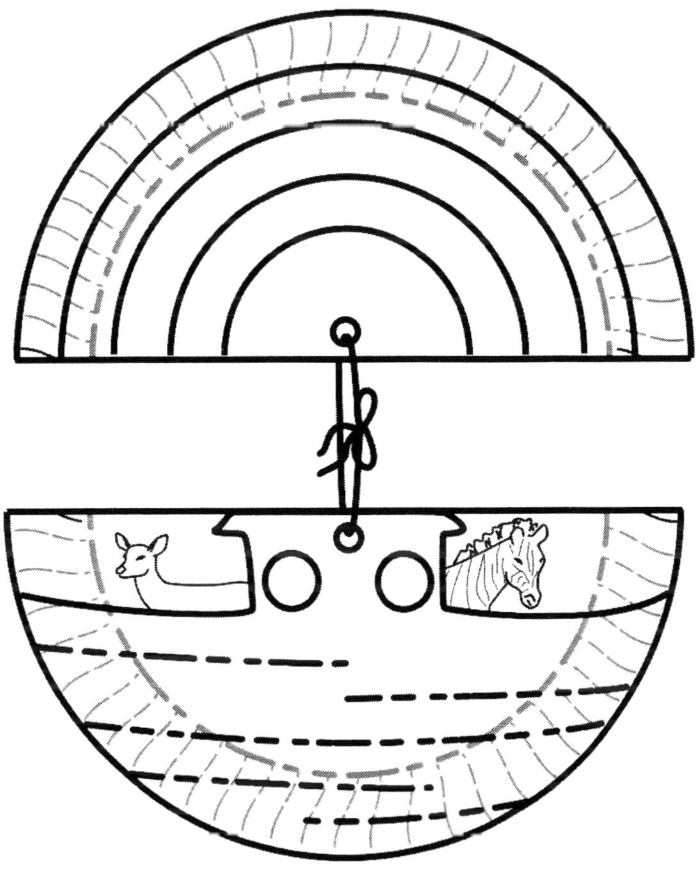

17. Nephi's Courage

Children's Songbook, 120

Opening Song: "Book of Mormon Stories," *Children's Songbook*, 118

Closing Song: "Nephi's Courage," *Children's Songbook*, 120

Materials Needed

- Gospel Art Picture # 303
- Primary 4-8 illustration
- One copy of the included illustrations on card stock
- Large piece of cardboard
- Heavy scissors or box knife
- Clear packing tape

Preparation

- Be familiar with the stories found in 1 Nephi 3–4 and 1 Nephi 17.
- Color and cut each illustration.
- Cut the cardboard into six, five to seven inch squares. Tape them together at right angles to form a cube.
- Tape one illustration on each face of the cube.

Teaching Suggestions

Most Primary children are familiar with this song, at least somewhat. This lesson is designed to reinforce the importance of the gospel stories and messages it contains, as well as add some new fun to this popular Primary song.

Begin by showing the children the picture of Nephi with the plates. Ask the children to help you tell the story the picture shows. Emphasize the importance of the job given to Nephi and his brothers and the trials they faced in fulfilling this command.

Ask the children what they would have done if they were Nephi. Why did Nephi keep trying?

Have them help you finish the story of how Nephi was able to get the plates. How do they think Nephi got in and out of the city? Nephi needed to be very cautious when he went to get the plates. He probably had to go very quietly to not draw attention to himself.

Tell the children that you will say the words to the first verse. Ask the children to whisper them back to you. Have them sing just the verse as quietly as they can. Tell them to pretend they are Nephi trying to get the plates.

Ask the children how Nephi felt about the job he was given to do. How would the children feel? Tell the children that even though Nephi didn't know what he was going to do, he trusted Heavenly Father to help him. He may have been a little nervous, but he promised to do what Heavenly Father asked, no matter what. He just went and did it.

Repeat the chorus for the children and then have them stand up and march in place as if they were going to do what the Lord asked while they repeat the chorus back to you.

Put the first verse and chorus together with the children whispering the verse and marching in rhythm to the chorus.

Ask the children to continue helping you tell the story of Nephi by remembering something else that Nephi was asked to do later. Heavenly Father asked him to build a boat to take his family to the promised land. Once again, Nephi was given a job to do, and he simply went to work.

Repeat the first two lines of this verse for the children and then invite them to gently pound the fist of one hand into the palm of the other hand, as if they were hammering, or building something. Have them do this in rhythm with the words as they say the lines back to you.

Next discuss Laman and Lemuel's behavior toward their brother and Heavenly Father's command. They laughed and teased Nephi for trying, and trusting in the Lord. State the next two lines of the second verse for the children. Then let them repeat it back to you in a loud, teasing voice.

Ask the children what happened to Laman and Lemuel when they teased Nephi (The Lord told Nephi to touch his brothers. The Lord shocked them. They were afraid and finally agreed to help Nephi). Show the gospel art picture #303. Allow the children to pop up and down from their seat when they say the word "do" as they repeat the chorus. Have the children sing the second verse and chorus with all three actions in place.

Move to the last verse. Assure the children that they can learn a lot about how to obey Heavenly Father and choose the right from Nephi's example. It's not always easy to choose the right, but Heavenly Father will always bless us when we are trying to do what He asks us to. Repeat the third verse for the children. Then allow them "choose another way." Tell them to turn around at their seats and repeat this verse back to you while facing the back of the room.

Help the children understand that even though they were doing something different, it does not represent a sin. It is just to remind us that we have lots of choices every day because Heavenly Father has given us agency. Some choices are tiny, and some are big. We need to make choices that are most pleasing to our Heavenly Father.

Show the children that all of the actions that were used in reviewing this song are mounted on your action cube. Begin with the first verse again. Invite a reverent child to come roll your cube to see how they will sing this verse of the song. Roll twice more for the other two verses. Then sing the song all the way through using the chosen action with each verse.

Nephi in Action Cube

- **Sneaking inside the city gate—**whisper
- **Go and Do**—marching
- **Build a boat**—hammer

- **Laughing and Mocking**—megaphone
- **Shocking Laman and Lemual**—pop up (straight arrow)
- **Choose another way**—turn around (curved arrow)

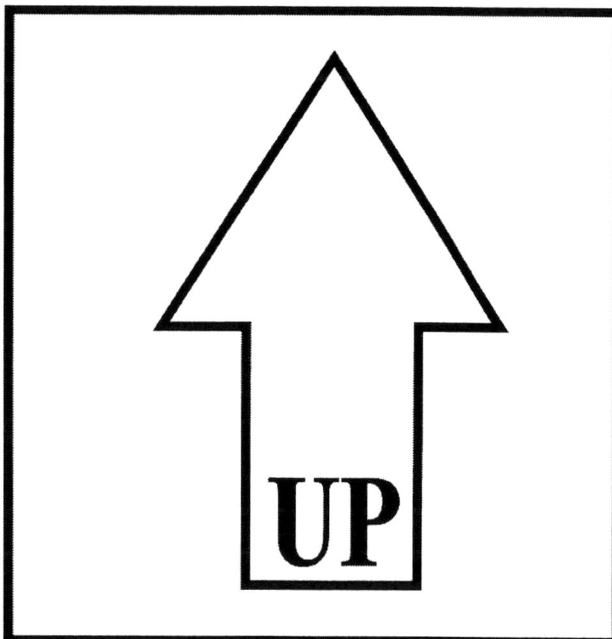
UP
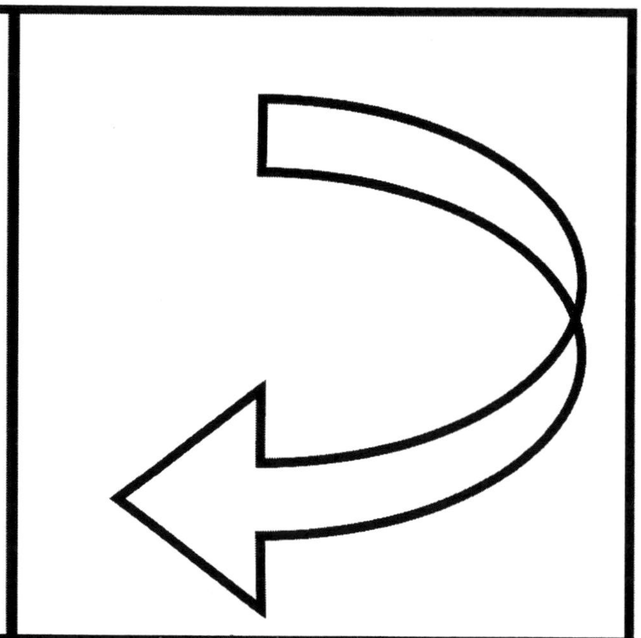

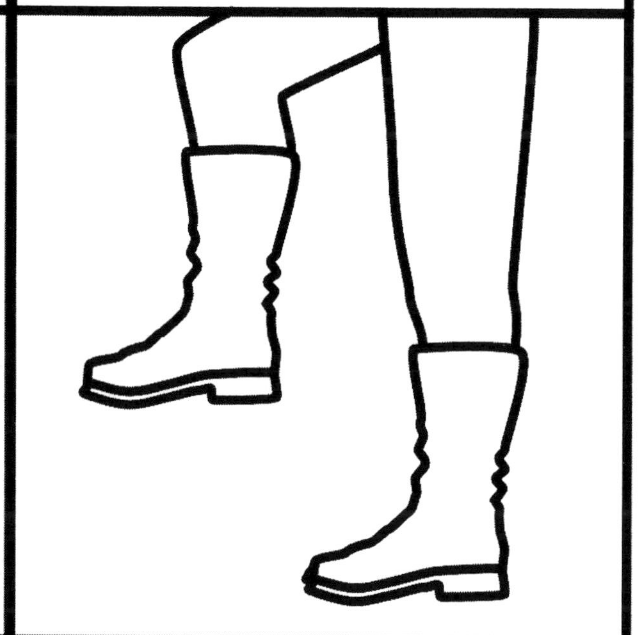

18. A Scripture Comforter

Opening Song: "I Feel My Savior's Love," *Children's Songbook*, 74

Closing Song: "Listen, Listen," *Children's Songbook*, 107

Materials Needed

- A large quilt or blanket
- Copies of the included illustrations
- Eight safety pins
- Hole punch
- Moveable chalkboard or large display area that will support the weight of the quilt
- Scriptures for use by children

Preparation

- Color, cut, and laminate the illustrations.
- Use the hole punch to make two holes at the top of each illustration with just a small amount of room between them. These will be used to pass the pin through for securing the picture to the blanket.

Teaching Suggestions

This lesson can be used as an overall review of the songs learned in preparation for your Primary program.

Show the children your quilt. Talk to them about what a quilt does. It offers warmth and comfort; it looks pretty or reminds us of someone or something special. Share with the children why your blanket has special meaning to you and the feelings you have when you enjoy its warmth.

Testify that the scriptures can also provide us with warmth and comfort. We can read in the scriptures about Heavenly Father and all the promises he has made to others to help them live the gospel. If we study the scriptures, we can receive comfort. We can know that Heavenly Father will bless us too. That is what He promises us.

Drape your blanket over the chalkboard. Have the children help you look up and read each scripture listed below. Help them understand the promise from the Lord found in each one. Sing the corresponding song. Then use a safety pin to secure each picture to the blanket to form a new "scripture comforter."

End with your testimony of the power of the scriptures and Heavenly Father's promises.

PICTURE, SCRIPTURE, AND SONG

- **Boy in armor**—Ephesians 6:11—"Scripture Power," *Friend,* October 1987, 10–11
- **Sheep**—Psalms 23:1–3—"I Know My Father Lives," *Children's Songbook*, 5
- **Noah**—Genesis 6:18–19—"Follow the Prophets," *Children's Songbook*, 110
- **Jesus**—D&C 76:22—"Did Jesus Really Live Again?" *Children's Songbook*, 64
- **Ten Commandments**—3 Nephi 22:13—"Holding Hands Around the World," *Friend*, July 2002, 44–45
- **Nephite Burden**—Mosiah 24:8–15—"Dearest Children, God is Near You," *Hymns,* no. 96
- **Esther**—Esther 4:11–17, 5:1–2—"Tell Me, Dear Lord," *Children's Songbook*, 176
- **Joseph Smith**—Joseph Smith–History 1:11–13—"Search, Ponder and Pray," *Children's Songbook*, 109

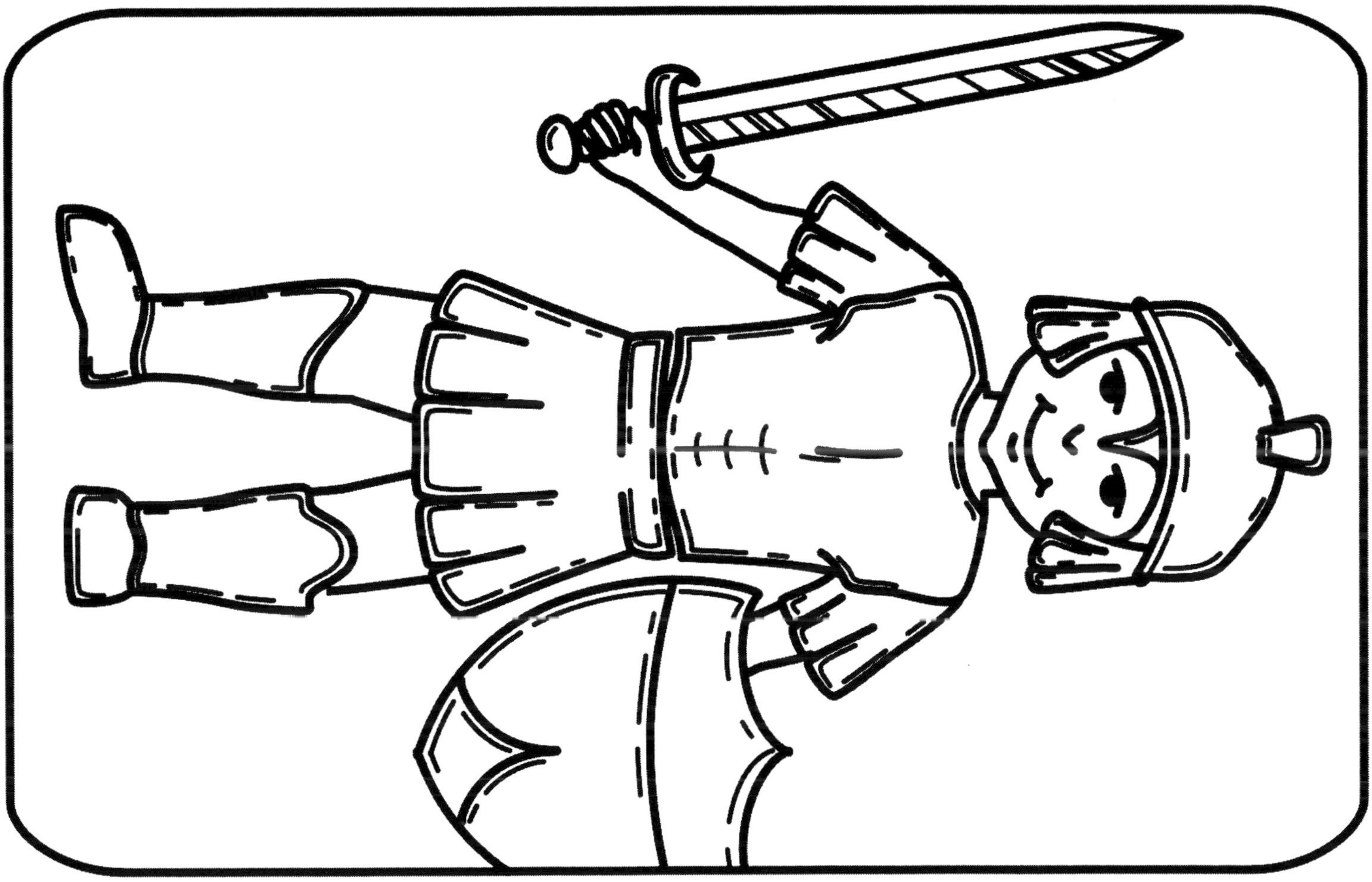

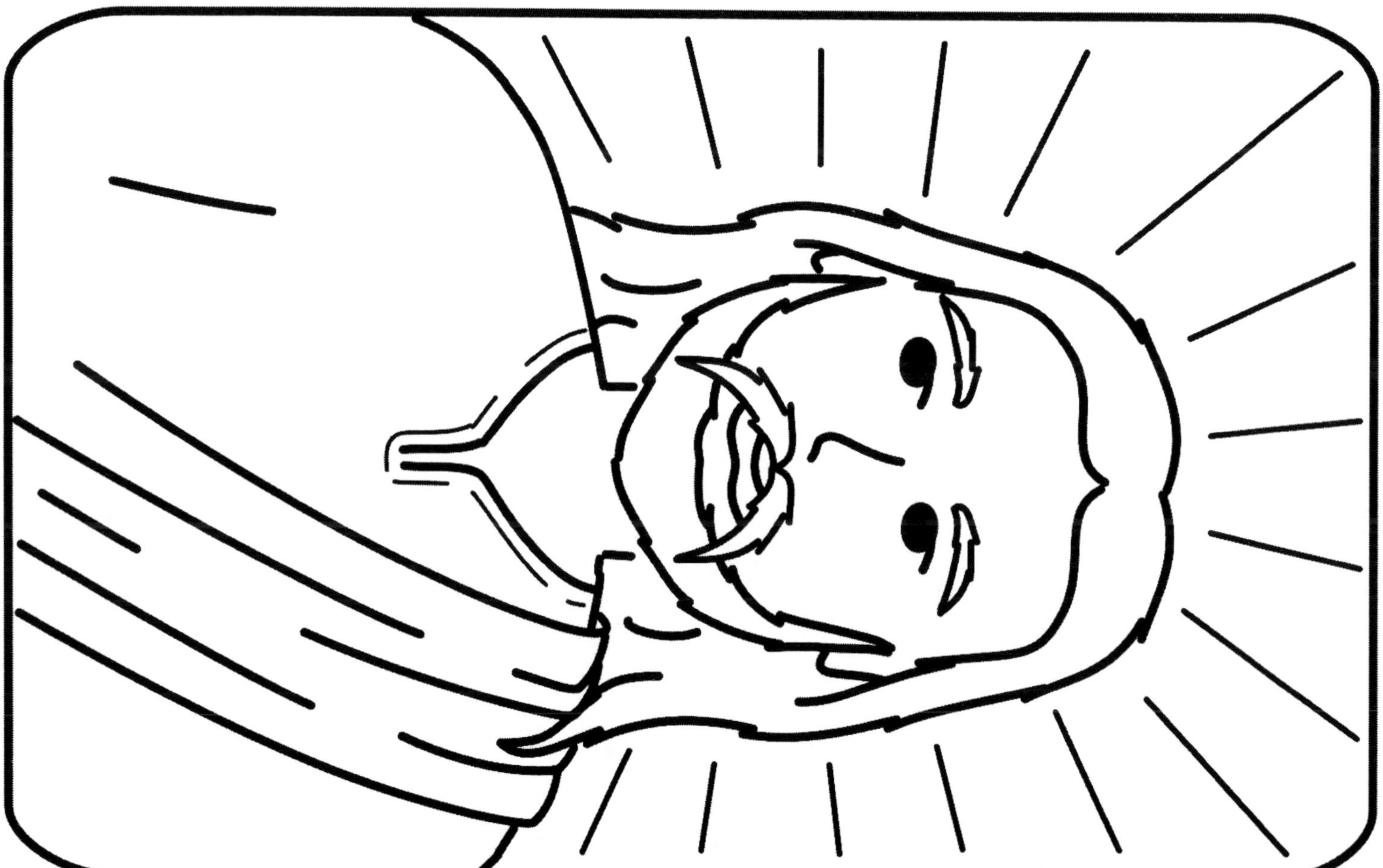

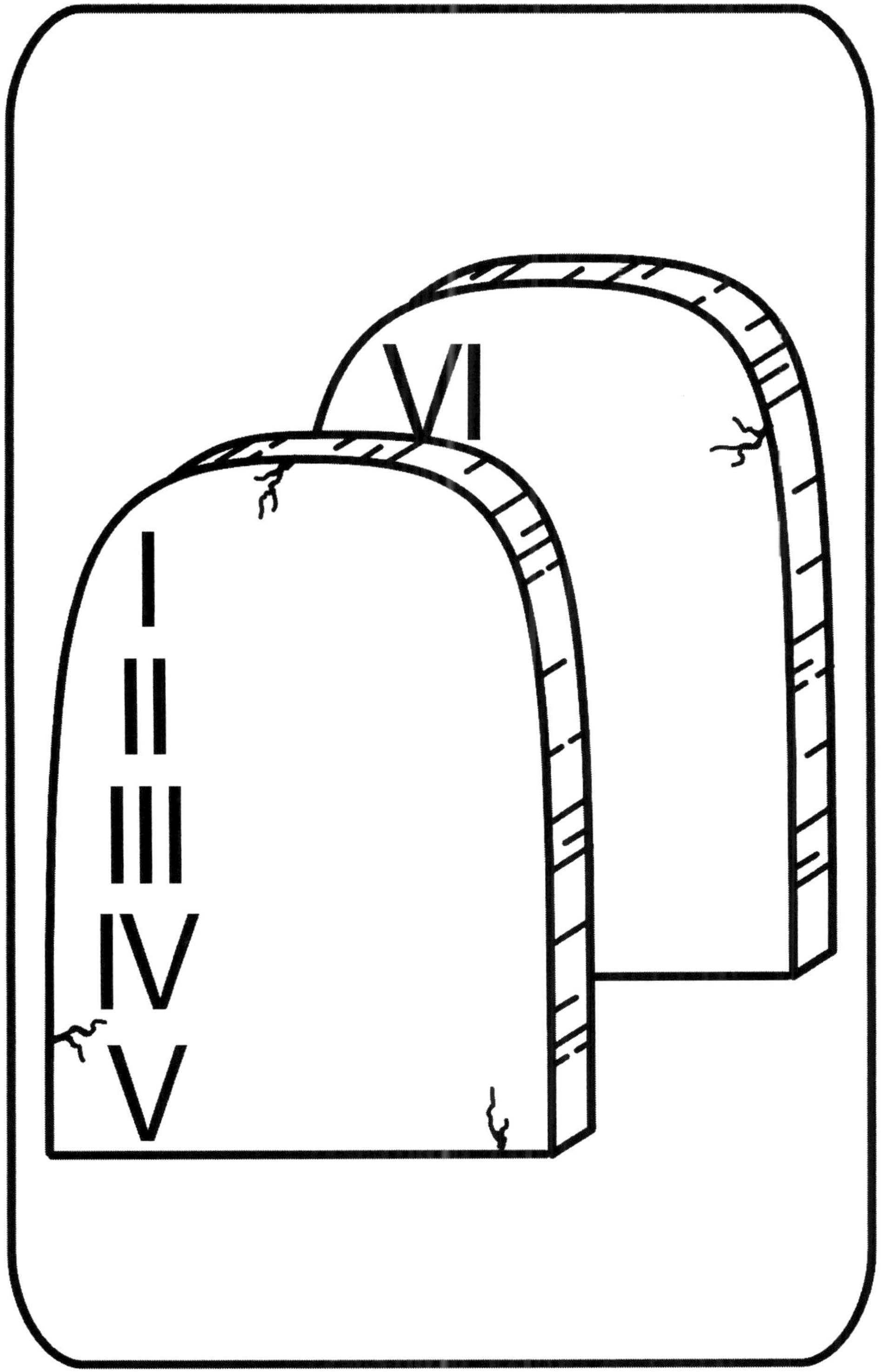
I
II
III
IV
V
VI

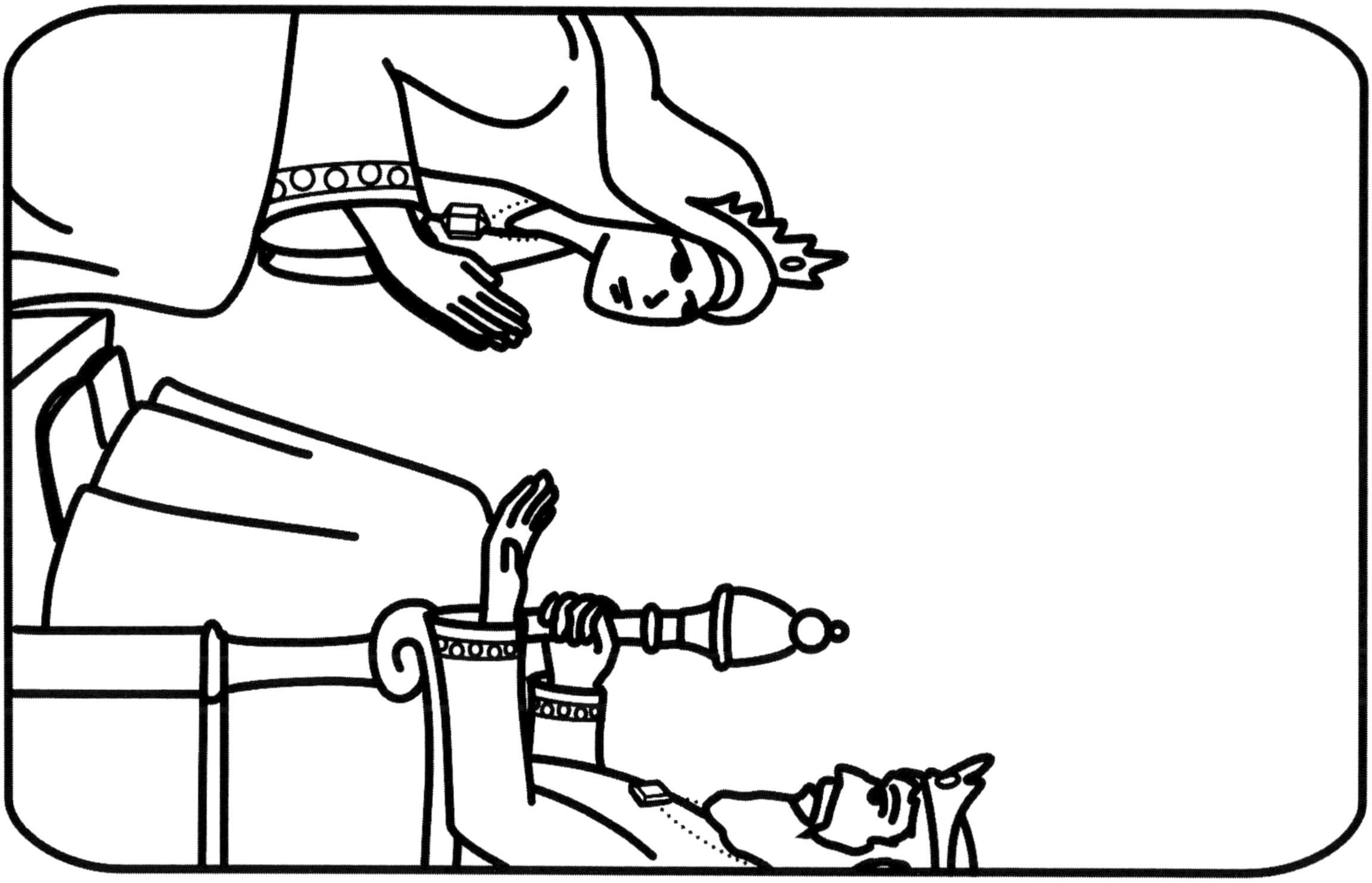

19. Keep the Commandments

Children's Songbook, 146

Opening Song: "I Will Follow God's Plan," *Children's Songbook*, 164

Closing Song: "Keep the Commandments," *Children's Songbook*, 146

Materials Needed

- Bible
- Chalkboard and chalk
- Gospel Art Pictures (prayerfully choose a few pictures from lessons you have covered during the year you would like to review with the children)

Preparation

- Write the following words on the chalkboard: commandments, safety, peace, blessings, prophet, children, tested, true, and promises.

Teaching Suggestions

Remind the children that they have been learning about Heavenly Father, and Jesus Christ's promises all year. They have also learned how they can make and keep promises with Heavenly Father and Jesus Christ. Ask the children to share some of the things they have learned.

Show the children your chosen gospel art pictures one at a time and have them help you describe what they learned from each story.

Heavenly Father wants to bless us. He has promised that He will be able to bless us when we are trying to be more like His son, Jesus Christ. That is why we have been given commandments and a living prophet to guide us. They help us to know what we can do so that Heavenly Father can be an important part of our lives.

The song they will learn today is to remind them of the important ways we try to remember to choose the right every day. The messages are very simple because Heavenly Father wants us to be able to understand.

Show the children the words you wrote on the board. Help them say each word with you.

Next, point to each word and ask the children to share their thoughts on what meanings this word could have. Commend the children for their thoughts about the gospel. Then share the song phrase associated with each word. Help the children repeat it back to you. Introduce the melody as you point to and sing the words for the children. Then let them sing the words back to you. Work through the entire song in this manner.

Bear your testimony of the gospel principles that the children have brought up and the need to try every day to be a little better by coming to understand Heavenly Father's commandments and the words of the prophets.

Ask the children to tell you where we can find the commandments that Heavenly Father wants us to keep. (His words are found in the scriptures.)

Tell the children that they will play a reverent version of hot potato while they practice this song. Remind the children that it is important for them to read the scriptures and understand what Heavenly Father wants them to be like. It is also important for them to share the things that they have learned with others. As the children practice singing "Keep the Commandments," they will gently pass the Bible around the room from child to child. The piano will periodically stop playing. The child found holding the Bible when the music stops must try to state the next line of the song that would have been sung. If he or she is successful, the singing begins from the point where it left off. If he or she is unable to identify the next line, the wording is reviewed and singing must begin again from the beginning. At first, the words on the board may be used to help prompt the children, but they should be removed as the children become more familiar with the song.

20. A Prophet Timeline

Opening Song: "Latter-day Prophets," *Children's Songbook*, 134

Closing Song: "Follow the Prophet," *Children's Songbook*, 110

Materials Needed

- Long piece of kite string or yarn—needs to be at least ninety inches long
- Gospel Art Pictures #107, 119, 216, 307, 312, 313, 500, 520, and 609
- Tape or other appropriate fasteners
- Ten spring-close clothespins
- Enlarged copy of the family illustration from "Choosing Happiness" (chapter 4) on cardstock

Preparation

- Review the stories of the different prophets (see the scriptures and other listed references) before presenting this lesson.
- Color the family picture.
- Mount the picture of the family at the front of the Primary room.
- Secure one end of the yarn just below the picture (tying it to something will work best, if possible) and leave the other end free.

Teaching Suggestions

Have one child be your helper. He or she will hold the free end of the string; it should be stretched out so that it is taut. (Helpers can be switched as the lesson progresses.)

Help the children understand that many prophets have shared stories and revelations that can help us have happier families. Today they will assemble a timeline that shows some of these different things.

Start at the end of string that is closest to the child holding it. Place pictures from the different prophet stories on the line, in order, using the clothespins to secure them to the string. Briefly discuss who the prophet was, what the picture represents, and what he taught us about families. Sing the song about each concept. Continue until all the prophets have been hung on the timeline, and you have reached the picture of the family.

Picture, Prophet, and Suggested Songs

1. Gospel Art Picture #119: **Adam and Eve**—Moses 5:10–12. Made the choices that allowed us to have families here on earth.

Sing: "Follow the Prophet," verse 1, *Children's Songbook*, 110

2. Gospel Art Picture #107: **Moses**—Exodus 20:12. Presented the Ten Commandments, especially "honor thy parents."

   Sing: "The Commandments," *Children's Songbook*, 112

3. Gospel Art Picture #307: **King Benjamin**—Mosiah 4:14–15. Instructed his people to teach their children about the gospel.

   Sing: "Teach Me to Walk in the Light," *Children's Songbook*, 177

4. Gospel Art Picture #312: **Alma**—Alma 43:47. Defend and protect your families.

   Sing: "Fathers," *Children's Songbook*, 209

5. Gospel Art Picture #313: **Helaman**—Alma 56:47–48, 57:26. Two thousand Stripling Warriors learned faith from their parents.

   Sing: "Book of Mormon Stories," verse 6, *Children's Songbook*, 118

6. Gospel Art Picture #216: **Jesus**—Mark 10:13–16. Showed us children are very special. How many other teachings/instances can the children name?

   Sing: "Jesus Loved the Little Children," *Children's Songbook*, 59

7. Gospel Art Picture #609: **Paul**—Colossians 3:18–21. The relationship of husbands and wives.

   Sing: "Love One Another," *Children's Songbook*, 136

8. Gospel Art Picture #500: **Joseph Smith**—D&C 132:18. Modern revelation for eternal families and the restoration of temple sealing.

   Sing: "Families Can Be Together Forever," *Children's Songbook*, 188

9. Gospel Art Picture #616: **Joseph F. Smith**—1915. Introduced the Family Home Evening program.

   Sing: "The Family," *Children's Songbook*, 194

10. Gospel Art Picture #520: **Gordon B. Hinckley**—1995. Introduced *The Family: A Proclamation to the World.*

    Sing: "Love is Spoken Here," *Children's Songbook*, 190

21. My Heavenly Father Loves Me

Children's Songbook, 228

Opening Song: "I Know My Father Lives," *Children's Songbook*, 5

Closing Song: "My Heavenly Father Loves Me," *Children's Songbook*, 228

Materials Needed

- Bird ornament/figurine
- Small piece of blue fabric
- Bottle of water
- Pinwheel
- Fabric rose
- Small branch from a tree
- Small globe
- Sunglasses or reading glasses
- Butterfly
- Headphones
- Small baby doll
- Picture of a child praying
- Heart
- Display table
- Two large tablecloths

Variations on the above objects can be made, as long as the association to the message is still clear.

Preparation

- Place one tablecloth on the display table.
- Arrange the above items on the table.

Teaching Suggestions

This lesson is an expression of thankfulness for all that Heavenly Father has given each of us.

Show the children your display table. Help them understand that each thing on the table represents a blessing that Heavenly Father has given us; these things show us how much He loves us. Ask the children to share what they are most thankful for.

Begin with the first phrase of the song. Show the children the corresponding item and state the words for the children. Then let them repeat the words back to you.

Move through all the items for the first verse in the same pattern. Then begin again. Hold up the items and let the children tell you what each phrase was.

Introduce the melody. Hold up each item in order and let the children sing through the first verse.

Repeat this process for the second verse.

After both verses have been sung about, tell the children that you will test their memory of the song by removing items from the table. Have another leader hold the second tablecloth over the table while you secretly remove one item. Then show the children the table again. The children must first tell you what item was removed and then what words were associated with that item. The verse including that item will be sung again with the children humming in place of the words represented by the item that was removed. That item will then be replaced and another removed, and so on.

Close with your testimony of all the wonderful things Heavenly Father has given us. If time remains, you might choose to give the children pencils and paper to illustrate their favorite blessing from Heavenly Father.

Materials and Associated Words

- **Bird ornament/figurine**—"Whenever I hear the song of a bird"
- **Small piece of blue fabric**—"Or look at the blue, blue sky,"
- **Bottle of water**—"Whenever I feel the rain on my face"
- **Pinwheel**—"Or the wind as it rushes by,"
- **Fabric rose**—"Whenever I touch a velvet rose"
- **Small branch from a tree**—"Or walk by our lilac tree,"
- **Small globe**—"I'm glad that I live in this beautiful world Heav'nly Father created for me."
- **Sunglasses or reading glasses**—"He gave me my eyes that I might see"
- **Butterfly**—"The color of butterfly wings."
- **Headphones**—"He gave me my ears that I might hear the magical sound of things."
- **Small baby doll**—"He gave me my life, my mind, my heart:"
- **Picture of child praying**—"I thank him rev'rently for all his creations, of which I'm a part."
- **Heart**—"Yes, I know Heav'nly Father loves me."

22. Treasures of the Gospel

Opening Song: "My Heavenly Father Loves Me," *Children's Songbook*, 228

Closing Song: "The Church of Jesus Christ," *Children's Songbook*, 77

Materials Needed

- Copy of the treasure chest illustration
- One package of multicolored craft jewels
- Small cloth sack or other nice container to hold the jewels
- Poster tack, double sided tape, or other fastener
- Multicolored construction paper
- Black marker
- Chalkboard or other display area

Preparation

- Color and laminate illustration.
- Match each jewel color with a same colored piece of construction paper. Write one scripture with its reference on each paper.
- Mount the treasure chest in the middle of the chalkboard.
- Mount the construction paper scriptures, face down, around the treasure chest.

Teaching Suggestions

Begin by sharing your testimony of the gospel with the children. Express the value you place on your testimony and the important truths that you have learned through the gospel.

Show the children your treasure chest and tell them that they will help you identify parts of the gospel that we should be grateful for and treat as special treasures.

Call reverent children up to remove jewels from your sack. The child will match the color of the jewel to the construction paper scripture. Read the scripture, briefly discuss the topic, then sing the song. Place the jewel on the treasure chest illustration and draw a new jewel until all the items have been identified.

If time remains, invite the children to think of other gospel "treasures" that could be added to your chest. Place an additional jewel for each new item they mention.

End with a second brief testimony.

GOSPEL TREASURES

- **Living Prophet**—Amos 3:7—"Latter-day Prophets," *Children's Songbook*, 134
- **Temples**—Micah 4:2—"I Love to See the Temple," *Children's Songbook*, 95
- **Book of Mormon**—Mosiah 1:7—"Book of Mormon Stories," *Children's Songbook*, 118
- **Priesthood**—The Fifth Article of Faith—"The Fifth Article of Faith," *Children's Songbook*, 125
- **Gospel Standards**—3 Nephi 27:21—"Keep the Commandments," *Children's Songbook*, 146
- **Word of Wisdom**—D&C 89:4—"The Word of Wisdom," *Children's Songbook,* 154
- **Plan of Salvation**—Moroni 7:41—"I Lived in Heaven," *Children's Songbook*, 4
- **Primary**—3 Nephi 22:13—"Our Primary Colors," *Children's Songbook*, 258
- **Family Home Evening**—Malachi 4:6—"The Family," *Children's Songbook*, 194
- **Missionary Work**—Matthew 28:19-20—"I Hope They Call Me on a Mission," *Children's Songbook*, 169

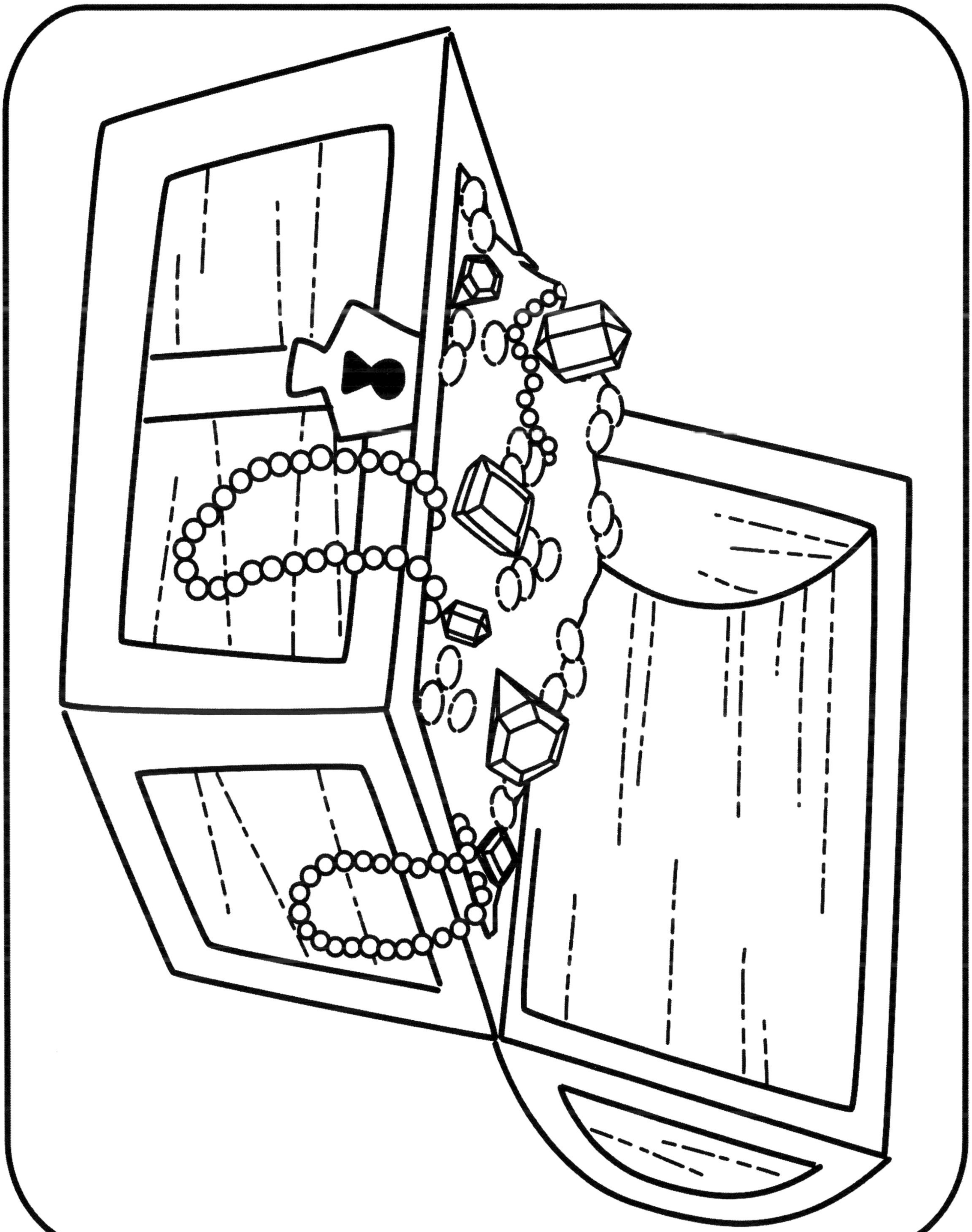

23. Samuel Tells of Baby Jesus

Children's Songbook, 36

Opening Song: "Book of Mormon Stories," *Children's Songbook*, 118

Closing Song: "Samuel Tells of Baby Jesus," *Children's Songbook*, 36

Materials Needed

- Several sets of scripture for children to use
- Gospel Art Picture #314
- Chalk and chalkboard
- Fifteen construction paper word strips

Preparation

- Write each scripture reference from below on a word strip.
- Write the words to this song on the board leaving space for the word strips to be placed, as illustrated on page 92.
- Place the appropriate scripture reference in each blank.
- For junior Primary, provide a list of the needed words at the bottom of the board to choose from.
- Review the story of Samuel's prophecy found in Helaman 13 and 14, and 3 Nephi 1:9–15.

Teaching Suggestions

Tell the children that the words on the board represent a very important prophecy that is found in the scriptures. When we read the scriptures, we learn about things that have happened and things that will still happen. We learn the messages that all the past prophets have prepared for us to hear.

Show the children the picture of Samuel. Ask them if they remember which prophet is being portrayed and what he might have said that they will be learning about today.

The children will help you fill in the blanks in this new song's lyrics. They will identify what important event is being talked about by reading their scriptures. Everywhere a scripture is posted in the song, a word is missing. If they read the scripture, they can figure out what word is missing.

Have the children begin with the first line and work through to the end of the song. Stop after every couple of phrases are completed. Repeat the words with the children introduce the melody, and allow the children to sing what they have learned to that point.

When the entire song has been sung, go back and share the entire story of Samuel's prophecy with the children.

End with your testimony of your knowledge of the importance of listening to the prophets' council, your knowledge that Heavenly Father will always keep His promises, and your thankfulness for the birth of the Savior.

LYRICS AND SCRIPTURE REFERENCES

Said Samuel "Within _______ **(Helaman 14:2)** years A _______ **(Helaman 14:3)** will be as _______. **(Helaman 14:3)** And Baby _______ **(Matthew 1:21)** will be born In a land far, far away."

_______! **(Matthew 21:9)** _______! **(Matthew 21:9)** Oh, let us gladly _______. **(Psalm 96:1)**
How blessed that our Lord was born; Let earth receive her _______! **(Zechariah 14:9)**
Across the sea, in _______ **(Matthew 2:1)** Lord _______ **(Matthew 1:21)** came to earth As Samuel had prophesied, And _______ **(Luke 2:13)** sang His birth.
_______! **(Matthew 21:9)** _______! **(Matthew 21:9)** Oh, let us gladly _______. **(Psalm 96:1)**
How blessed that our Lord was born; Let earth receive her _______! **(Zechariah 14:9)**

24. A PROMISE IN NATIVITY

Opening Song: "I Feel My Savior's Love," *Children's Songbook*, 74

Closing Song: "The Nativity Song," *Children's Songbook*, 52

MATERIALS NEEDED

- Table top nativity set (note: do not choose one with more than twelve pieces, or eliminate extra pieces so that the messages you feel are most important can be portrayed)
- Scriptures for children to use
- Table with cloth for displaying the nativity
- Masking tape
- Pen

PREPARATION

- Mark the bottom of each piece in your nativity set with small piece of tape. Number the pieces one through twelve.
- Prayerfully study the scripture options listed below and match them to your pieces of nativity. Adjust scriptures as needed. Number the scriptures used so that they match the number given to that piece of your nativity.
- Place Nativity set on the table, but do not set it up.

TEACHING SUGGESTIONS

A Nativity set is a beautiful way to remember Jesus' birth. We can also remember the ways we can promise to follow Jesus Christ when we look at a nativity scene. Each piece can tell us about something we should do if we want to be like Jesus.

Reverent children will be called up to choose a piece of the nativity scene. The scripture reference for that piece is read and briefly discussed. The appropriate song is sung. Place the piece is the appropriate spot in the scene. Placement continues until the scene is complete.

End with your testimony of the birth of the Savior and His life. Encourage the children to look closely at each nativity scene they see this season and quietly resolve which piece they would like to be. Promise them that as they promise to be more like Jesus Christ every day, blessings will follow and they will feel the same peace in their lives that looking at a nativity scene can bring.

NATIVITY PIECES AND SCRIPTURAL REFERENCES

- **Baby Jesus**—John 13:15 (follow Jesus' example)—"Jesus Once was a Little Child," *Children's Songbook*, 55
- **Mary**—Luke 1:26–27 (kept herself clean and pure)—"The Lord Gave Me a Temple," *Children's Songbook*, 153; Luke 1:46–47 (found joy in serving God)—"I Will Follow God's Plan," *Children's Songbook*, 164
- **Joseph**—1 Nephi 1:1 (learning from goodly parents)—"Teach Me to Walk in the Light," *Children's Songbook*, 177
- **Manger**—Luke 2:7 (we can always make room in our lives for someone in need)—"I'll Walk with You," *Children's Songbook*, 140
- **Shepherd**—Luke 2:15–16 (acting with haste to do what the Lord wants us to do)—"I Will Be Valiant," *Children's Songbook*, 162; Psalms 23:1 (the Lord will provide us with peace and guidance if we follow Him)—"I Feel My Savior's Love," *Children's Songbook*, 74
- **Sheep**—John 21:17 (feed my sheep)—"The Things I Do," *Children's Songbook*, 170; John 10:27 (hear my voice)—"I Think When I Read That Sweet Story," *Children's Songbook*, 56; John 10:16 (recognize everyone is a child of God and loved by Him)—"Children All Over the World," *Children's Songbook*, 16
- **Cattle**—Isaiah 11:6 (be a peacemaker, love our enemies)—"Kindness Begins with Me," *Children's Songbook*, 145
- **Camel**—Matthew 19:24 (be unselfish and giving)—"'Give,' Said the Little Stream," *Children's Songbook*, 236
- **Wiseman**—Colosians 13:16 (word of Christ is wisdom, scripture study)—"Scripture Power," *Friend,* October 1987, 10–11; James 1:5 (prayer)—"I Pray in Faith," *Children's Songbook*, 14; Mosiah 2:36 (Spirit guides in wisdoms path, Holy Ghost)—"The Holy Ghost," *Children's Songbook*, 105
- **Angel**—Alma 29:1–2 (joy of missionary work)—"We'll Bring the World His Truth," *Children's Songbook*, 172
- **Donkey**—Mosiah 18:8–10 (bear one another's burdens)—"We Are Different," *Children's Songbook*, 263
- **Star**—Matthew 5:16 (let your light so shine)—"Jesus Wants Me for a Sunbeam," *Children's Songbook*, 60

About the Author

Alison Palmer is a lifelong member of the Church. Born in Mesa, Arizona, she grew up in West Virginia and graduated from Marshall University with a bachelor's degree in nursing.

Alison has held many callings in the Church, including several that have helped develop her great love for Primary children. She has served as nursery leader, pianist, chorister, teacher, den leader, and Primary president. She has also taught Sunday School and served as a teacher and leader in the Relief Society and Young Women organizations.

Writing is Alison's favorite pastime, but you can frequently find her reading, playing piano, cooking, attending the temple, taking long walks, sewing, or playing with her family.

Alison is the author of *Sharing through Song Volume One, Planting Seeds of Faith: Fun Character-building Activities for LDS Children,* and *Walking the Path of Faith: More Fun Character-building Activities for LDS Children.*

You can learn more about Alison and visit with her at www.ampalmer.com.

0 26575 07980 7